MINIATURE AUSTRALIAN SHEPHERD

OWNER'S MANUAL

HOW TO CARE, TRAIN, AND KEEP YOUR MINI AUSSIE
HEALTHY. INCLUDES MINIATURE AMERICAN
SHEPHERD INFORMATION.

Acknowledgements

I would like to thank my wife and children for their patience whilst writing this book. Australian Shepherds have always been part of our household, and today we also share it with Kara, our very own Mini Aussie. I have always been inspired by their unfailing love and dedication to our family, something that I could never hope to repay. Although a ball and tug rope certainly helps.

★ Veterinarian Approved Content ★

This book has been reviewed by our own veterinary surgeon, and approved for its health related content. However, always check with your own vet before using any information provided in this book, as there are different canine healthcare requirements around the world.

This book is not intended as a substitute for the medical advice of a veterinarian. The reader should regularly consult a veterinarian in matters relating to their dogs health and particularly with respect to any symptoms that may require diagnosis or medical attention.

The Essentials

Table of Contents

Introduction

Welcome to a wealth of advice on the wonderful Miniature Australian Shepherd dog. This little Aussie is rapidly becoming a firm favorite in agility and canine sport circles.

They have all the drive of their bigger relatives, the standard sized Australian Shepherd, yet are a more compact package, which will give them a distinct advantage in many dog sports. They even have the natural ability to excel in an air-scenting, search and rescue lifestyle.

Their popularity is spreading way beyond that of competition, and towards being a great pet for an active home or family. They need a busy life and will repay you with high intelligence, unending loyalty and a vast learning capacity.

Whether you have picked up this book to learn how to train your Mini Aussie, want to learn more about the breed and their needs, or are having a problem with your existing dog, then read on.

We will cover everything you need to know. From playtime to puppies, clicker training to neutering, and everything in between nestles right here. All the information you can think of is covered in these pages.

In this book we go way beyond instructions about these delightful dogs. We delve into a canine understanding that will serve you for many years to come.

We show you how and why your dog behaves the way it does, and give you the tools to create and maintain the best ever relationship with your Miniature Australian Shepherd.

Section 1: Get to Know the Breed

This section of the book should really be compulsive reading for anyone considering bringing home a dog that has a strong working ancestry, with the drive and high energy levels that go with it.

Pet dogs from herding ancestry, are often chosen for their looks, natural obedience and general good manners. Sadly, without research into the breed and preparation for the specific needs of any dog, the match between home and breed can easily fail. Many dogs end up homeless as they pass through adolescence for exactly this reason.

It is easy to bring home a herding dog and expect it to cope with the same amount of mental and physical exercise as a dog bred only to act as a companion.

A Shih Tzu, as a random example, was bred to sit on laps and keep their human company. The small Shih Tzu is happy with a daily wander to the park and some cuddles, or to learn the odd trick.

An Australian Shepherd dog has other needs. This dog was bred to do something completely different. If the Aussie, regardless of its size, is expected to cope with the same exercise levels as the Shih Tzu, on a long-term basis, then they will develop behavioral problems.

During this first section of the book we are going to share exactly what the needs of the Mini Aussie are, why they are so, and how they have been bred to accentuate certain behaviors, thus creating these particular needs.

This section of the book is the first step to your perfectly complete understanding of the Miniature Australian Shepherd. Read on and enjoy!

What is a Mini Australian Shepherd?

What is the difference between an Australian Shepherd dog and its smaller relative? In all honesty there is very little difference at all.

The Miniature Australian Shepherd is all Aussie. They were bred from the standard sized Australian Shepherd dog to be a smaller and more compact version of the original breed.

No other dog breed was introduced in order to make the Mini Aussie so small, so they have as much drive and working dog personality as their larger ancestors, making them wonderful dogs for a high energy and active lifestyle.

How should the Mini Australian Shepherd look?

The height of the Mini Aussie, to be differentiated from the standard Australian Shepherd, is to range between 35 and 46 cm from ground to withers (the ridge between the shoulder blades).

Their weight should be between 9 and 14 kg. The Mini Aussie has the same range of coat colors as the larger dog. They can be black and white, red, blue or red merle, and any of these colors can have coppery hints.

Like other herding breeds, the Mini Aussie can have a range of eye colors including hazel, blue, brown and amber, and can even have two different colored eyes. They can though suffer from eye problems, which we will talk more about later.

The Mini Aussie is also a dog that unfortunately suffers from the tendency of humans to tail dock (cutting off their tails). This practice is illegal for reasons other than health in the UK. Animal welfare groups are also petitioning to make it illegal in the US, however so far it is unrestricted.

Tail docking used to be popular with the breed because some Australian Shepherds are naturally born with bobbed tails or mid-size ones. This was regarded as a useful trait when herding large animals, where their tails could easily be trodden on and damaged. Today, as you are unlikely to find cows roaming around in city parks, the need to dock tails is no longer necessary.

Life Expectancy:

Mini Aussies have an average life span of 12-13 years, however it is not uncommon for many live for a few years beyond this. So you will have plenty of time for games in the park, or walks in the hills together.

History:

The Miniature Australian Shepherd, despite their name, actually originates from North America, and as a result some breeders prefer to call them the Miniature American Shepherd, as is discussed in the next chapter.

A lady called Doris Cordova bred the first smaller Aussie, within a program that began in the late 1960s. Doris worked alongside a veterinary surgeon in order to create and carry out a successful breeding program.

The dogs that she used in the program were Australian Shepherd dogs, chosen specifically for their smaller size. They were shipped over to Doris in California and eventually she had created a new breed by artificial selection. The Miniature Australian Shepherd was born.

As we know of its history so far, the Mini Aussie is simply an Australian Shepherd dog in petite form, bred from smaller standard Aussies until they reached a size that was deemed appropriate to be labeled Miniature. In the 1980s specific Mini Aussie clubs were eventually formed.

The full size Australian Shepherd dog has a relatively vague history, however it is generally believed that they came from the Basque regions of Spain where they were used by shepherds, eventually emigrating with their owners to the USA via Australia.

The Miniature American Shepherd

The Mini American Shepherd is, in reality, exactly the same as our Mini Aussie. Any confusion occurs, not with the dog type but with the name.

In actual fact, because the first Mini Aussie was bred in North America breeders are (to a point) within their rights to call them a Mini American Shepherd. Though they do descend from the standard Aussie that arrived in the US, from Australia, sometime in the 1800's.

The Kennel Club

As we know, development of the dog began in the 1960's with Doris. They were bred directly from the Australian Shepherd dog to be small yet still hardy and driven. They were then still called the Mini Australian Shepherd and this was deemed the future name of the breed. Yet with kennel club regulations this was not to be.

When the Mini Australian Shepherd Club of America formed in 1990, they were disallowed to register their relatively new breed. This is because the Australian Shepherd was also registered in the same year as a breed, and the similarity was too great. This application for registration left the kennel club in a quandary and eventually they requested The Mini Australian Shepherd Club of America change its name in order to register their breed.

The club became The Mini American Shepherd Club of America, keeping its acronym. They now have the status as a separate breed to the Australian Shepherd.

The Facts

- The Australian Shepherd is registered with the American Kennel club simply as an Australian Shepherd dog with no size variation.

- There is actually now another Mini Australian Shepherd club of America and there are specific breeders of the Mini Aussie but they exist for the love of the breed and state that are not concerned about kennel club status beyond that of the Australian Shepherd Dog with size variation.
- The Australian Shepherd club of the UK states that they do not support the breeding of Mini Aussies nor American shepherd dogs as a member of the Australian Shepherd breed.
- The UK Kennel club only recognizes the Australian Shepherd as a registered breed within the pastoral group.

So the mini Aussie is unrecognized and unacknowledged by the aforementioned clubs. Does this matter?

As a dog lover, and owner, I wanted to let you know the background behind the name confusion. In reality, as long as the dog is healthy, well-bred and suitable for your lifestyle it really doesn't matter what the various clubs think. Kennel clubs have actually earned their own criticisms over the last few years in regards to the health of many dogs involved in their breeding guidelines.

The thing to remember is that the two breeds are in fact the same - and the only choice that you have to make is whether to bring home one bred as a Miniature American Shepherd that you can register (with the American Kennel Club), or a Mini Aussie that you may not be able to officially register but is the same dog nonetheless.

The Toy and Teacup Australian Shepherd

So what is a toy sized Aussie and what about a teacup dog? Well, the very small Australian Shepherd, purposely bred to be below the aforementioned Miniature Australian Shepherd sizes, is a product of unethical breeding.

Whilst the Miniature Aussie maintains a lot of the standard sized Aussies health and working attitude, like any breed that becomes popular, there are people that want to make money from them.

The toy and teacup Australian Shepherds are created by taking the smaller sized Miniature Australian Shepherd to the extreme. This type of genetic engineering is not popular with ethical breeders.

When a dog is bred to be very small, then they can also be very unhealthy. A dog that is reduced in size through selective breeding can suffer with fine bones that break easily. They can also struggle to excess with the general health problems of their breed.

The Miniature Aussie is a dog that has been carefully chosen and bred to be a strong and robust working dog, yet typically smaller than their original ancestor. Toy and teacup Aussies contradict this by making the smaller dog more delicate and less able to carry out the jobs that they were bred for.

Even companion dogs that have been bred to toy and teacup sizes have health problems, and to force such a reduction in size onto a dog with working heritage is grossly unfair.

So if you are thinking of purchasing an even smaller version of the Miniature Aussie, it is important to be well aware of the risks involved when deciding on a much smaller dog than the breed was ever intended to be. I am personally against the breeding of such dogs.

An Aussie Personality

The Miniature Aussie, when bred properly, has the nature of the working Australian Shepherd. They are easily trained plus interesting to work and live with.

They have high-energy and keenness to be busy most of the time - this is because in every intricate detail of their personality this dog is a working dog.

They are also becoming highly popular in competitive agility and obedience. They will excel at flyball and other sports, and as such they won't be happy in a quiet home without something to do.

As a herder, the Aussie can develop a tendency to actually herd people. This includes children, and they may even nip to try and bring playing children under control. This is an instinctive behavior that can be easily controlled with training.

For new owners, the exercise of having to deal with such herding traits, at some point, must be expected if you are thinking of bringing home a Miniature Aussie as a family pet. We will cover this behavior in more detail later in the book.

If their exercise levels are met and they receive enough activity to stimulate their complex mind, the Australian Shepherd in Miniature will be an easy dog to live with in the home. If they have excess energy, due to sitting around with nothing to do, the Aussie can develop behavior problems in and outside the home, which we will also talk about later.

As a companion they are very loyal and will bond strongly to their human family. They will throw themselves wholeheartedly into any activity that they are introduced to. However, they are also prone to becoming overly attached to their owners, so the Mini Aussie can also develop separation anxiety.

The ideal home for this dog is a dog trainer with a working dog background, a family that is dedicated to training and meeting all of their needs plus walking for at least a couple of hours a day, or someone that is looking for a dog to take to agility or another similar sport.

If you would like to share a busy life with a highly intelligent, superbly loyal and gentle dog then this little Aussie may be just the one for you.

Potential Health Issues

The Australian Shepherd, in comparison to other breeds, when bred properly, is generally healthy. The Miniature Aussie if carefully bred will carry the same robust physical health.

The main problem that this type of dog can suffer from are conditions of the eye.

They can develop early cataracts from as young as two years old. Other eye conditions include sensitivity to bright light, night blindness, early degeneration of the tissue in the lens, and a cleft that can be present in the iris, right from birth.

Eye problems are caused primarily by poor breeding. They can also be unforeseen genetic throwbacks from previous generations.

Sometimes breeders try to genetically engineer a specific version of the dog, by breeding a merle colored shepherd with another merle. This is because the color is popular with buyers, yet not common in natural breeding. Eye problems and even blindness is a regular risk with a double merle mating.

An ethical breeder will not consider this type of breeding.

With the Mini Aussie, hip dysplasia can also be a risk. A good breeder will hip check any dog that they plan to breed from. They will not take the risk of breeding a litter of Mini Aussies if the result was the majority developing hip problems.

A luxation of the patella is also a risk. This is where the kneecap slips as the dog walks. The kneecap will constantly click which can often be heard as the dog is walking. Some dogs have this rectified by surgery, whilst others manage quite well without an operation.

The final thing to look out for with a Mini Aussie is the universal allergy and negative response that the herding dog can have towards chemicals. Some medications, including parasite control, can cause a severe reaction within the breed.

It is therefore vital that before a Mini Aussie is given any kind of treatment, the medication is checked for possible allergic reactions and sensitivity. The response to some medications can be so severe that it proves fatal to the dog.

The other thing that herding breeds, and in fact a lot of dog breeds can suffer from, is genetic deafness. This is usually the effect of a merle-to-merle breeding, which as previously discussed, is highly discouraged.

If you have the time, canine genetics is a very interesting topic, and if you are thinking of getting a new puppy, worth the time researching. The genes that work out how the dog will look and act tend to 'hang around' in seemingly unrelated groups. One of these groups of genes, it has been discovered, has the effect of canine deafness in a high number of pure white dogs.

The deafness gene literally comes along with the gene that causes the dog to be pure white, in exactly the same way the gene that causes genetic eye problems is prominent in the breeding between two merle dogs. So therefore, if someone is trying to specifically breed white or merle puppies, they are ultimately breeding unhealthy dogs.

Therefore, unless a pure white or merle Mini Aussie is a complete accident in a litter of otherwise healthy colors, it is most certainly an unethical breeding. This is an interesting fact to consider when looking for your new dog, wouldn't you say?

Section 2: Find and Choose Your Mini Aussie

As a relatively new breed type (size wise) the Miniature Australian Shepherd is not yet as widely available as some other breeds of dog. Thus they are usually, and thankfully, found in the care of breeders that really understands and wants to preserve the breed.

There are however certain things to keep in mind when you are looking for a Mini Aussie. It is important that you know how to look for potential problems, plus how any puppy can be affected by poor breeding and negative early learning.

So during this section of the book we are going to talk through the following: puppy learning stages, the risk of choosing a poor dog breeder, and whether an adult dog could be a better choice for you.

We will also talk through the act of bringing the dog into your family with minimal upheaval, how you can introduce a dog of any age to your children, and why most dogs of this breed will live happily with any other pet that you have in the home.

We aim to answer all of your questions on choosing the right dog, and even some questions that you may not even have thought of yet.

A Puppy

A lot of people, when they decide on a dog for the home, think that a puppy is the best option. Some people even believe that a puppy is the only option.

It is easy to believe that if you bring home an eight-week old puppy, you can shape them into the adult that you would like them to be. This is true in many ways, however puppies are like babies and need as much care as any human child if they are to grow up confident and happy.

Puppies are learning from every interaction that you share with them. Whether you intend to be teaching them or not, they are learning nonetheless.

The Miniature Australian Shepherd puppy is highly intelligent and will actually learn quicker than many other breeds. Therefore it's really not a good idea to bring home a puppy of this breed and expect not to put lots of effort into his or her development.

In general, a puppy will need constant and consistent attention as they grow. They will pee in the house at the beginning, and so they will need to be taught exactly how you would like them to behave. If you do not carefully show an Aussie how to behave, then they will be more than happy to teach themselves bad habits.

They may also keep you up for the first few nights upon arrival at your home, like any new baby. So you are, from that moment on, completely responsible for how they grow up.

That said, the puppy is cute, happy, and an exciting addition to the home. Some people wait for years, carefully biding their time before bringing home a puppy. Others do it on a whim, and in this case can end up unable to cope with the dog a few months later.

So if you want a Miniature Australian Shepherd puppy, then you will also need to be prepared to take on the responsibility of shaping their behavior as they grow.

Remember this will be a baby in a new household, of a completely different species, that doesn't even speak their language.

The puppy will need all the help it can get.

Puppy Learning Stages and why they Matter

Puppy learning stages are absolutely fascinating and completely relevant to the potential owner of any dog. This is because every stage that the puppy passes through when they are learning develops their character as an adult dog.

The puppy begins to learn and develop in the womb. If its mother suffers from anxiety or negative treatment while she's pregnant, the puppy is subjected to, and will absorb hormones that shape their character as an older dog. Isn't that amazing?

A confident mother dog that is happy when pregnant, and is neither scared nor anxious, will usually give birth to more confident puppies. This is more the rule, but there are exceptions.

Another way that a puppy's behavior can be shaped whilst they are still in the womb is by male or female hormones. For instance, a solitary male dog developing within a litter of females will receive more female hormones; therefore their behavior will be more feminine as it grows. A solitary female will in turn develop an outlook similar to male dogs.

Despite their learning being highly affected by their environment, puppies are also born with some instinctive behaviors. The Australian Shepherd puppy has been finely tuned over many generations to be a dog that works as a herder. Therefore as they grow they will show an ability to learn quickly and even to herd, although sometimes this is shown in odd ways.

Because the Miniature Australian Shepherd is literally a herder in miniature, and has not been crossed with another dog breed, you will undoubtedly see the genetic traits that have been bred into them for many years.

They will also show independent thinking because the breed, as a working dog, had to think independently in order to perform its duties as a useful addition to caring for a flock of sheep.

Generic Puppy Learning

After they are born all puppies learn from both their mother's behavior and also the world around them. They learn in the following stages:

Neonatal Stage

Neonatal learning occurs in the period between puppy birth and twelve days. It can be difficult to believe that these tiny blind and deaf babies are actually learning enough to shape their characters.

Whilst they wriggle around the nesting area, usually either feeding or sleeping, they can actually taste and smell. They are also sensitive to pain, pressure, and touch.

The puppies during this stage also learn to recognize the scent of their mother's saliva. A mother dog will lick around her own nipples to show the puppy where their food comes from and also around the muzzles of her babies in order to introduce herself.

They also have the ability to use their heat-seeking nose to locate their mother if they are moved away from her.

Puppies at this age are only showing the types of behavior that ask for care. They make small sounds and only feed or toilet when their mother prompts them to.

With research showing that puppies can learn a lot during this stage, many organizations now suggest handling them carefully for short periods of time. It has been shown that slight pressure or temperature change during this period, will actually help the puppy to cope with other stressors as they grow up.

Despite their brain having barely developed, even the youngest puppy can, and will learn during the neonatal stage. In fact, the learning that they do during this period takes its own place in the development of a puppy's brain.

It has also been shown that puppies that experience careful handling during this stage, will develop coordination and the ability to move quicker than those that don't.

Transition Period of Puppy Learning

From day thirteen of the puppy's life, they enter a transition period. This is a period of quick change with the puppy, leaving behind the helplessness of its neonatal stage and beginning to move around.

At around thirteen days old a puppy's eyes will open but its vision will not be completely efficient until a few days after that.

From two weeks old the puppy will usually happily bottle feed and even begin to lap food if it is offered. This is normally a messy affair.

During this transition stage, a litter of puppies will begin to use their natural social behaviors to communicate amongst themselves. This communication is essential learning. The puppy will learn to wag its tail when feeling content and start to show other basic communication behaviors.

It will also begin to learn bite inhibition from both its mother and other puppies in the litter.

Bite inhibition is the knowledge and awareness of the damage that can be done with a bite. The mother dog and siblings will protest if a puppy bites too hard when playing or feeding. These protests come as a sharp noise or corrective body language.

It is highly important that every dog is given the chance to learn bite inhibition. For if the puppy is placed in a position when they are older, that it sees no opportunity for safety other than to bite, they therefore will be careful about how hard they do actually bite.

The Australian Shepherd dog is, as a herder, slightly more reactive than some other breeds. The nipping behavior when herding is a sign of reactivity. Due to this reactivity this breed of dog may be pushed to respond with a bite more quickly. Therefore it is highly important that the Aussie puppy receives its natural bite inhibition training.

The transition period is a time where the puppy learns a lot. By day twenty, the puppy's ear canals are open, so they can both see and hear.

Social Learning Period

This social learning period, or socialization period, is critical to a puppy. At the end of the transition period, and at around four weeks old, their environment really begins to shape them and their behavior.

Any learning or even lack of social contact during this stage cannot be undone. It is almost like the neurons that are developing within the puppy's brain, form directly from the environment around them.

A puppy that learns to be scared during the period between four and twelve weeks will undoubtedly take the fear behavior into their adulthood.

So, you bring a puppy home from a breeder at around eight weeks old. The first four weeks are in the breeders care, alongside its mother, and the last four weeks of this crucial learning period in your home.

Everything that happens to the puppy, in both places, decides how it's going to cope with life. It may be really traumatized by an event that you don't even notice and may seem no worse off afterwards. Yet this learning will stay in its mind and affect how it feels about the world later in its life.

Positive socialization is the key factor of a puppy's development during this stage. The dog that is totally removed from any contact with other dogs, at any point between the ages of four weeks and twelve weeks, will always be a little worried around other dogs. They will also not learn how to communicate properly with other dogs, which will add to its fear.

For the above reason alone it is vital that a puppy is allowed regular contact with other dogs. This will ensure both their own well being, as well as being able to learn good canine manners, communication, and how to display and read the body language that all dogs need if they are to be happy.

Puppies also need canine playtime, and to deny them this is quite unkind.

If you have ever seen a dog that seems to show aggression towards other dogs when on a lead, or that runs up over-enthusiastically and bounces all over the other dog, despite continuous canine warnings, then you have seen the results of a lack of positive socialization.

Soon we will talk about why it is really important to find a good breeder if you are considering a Miniature Australian Shepherd puppy. We will also talk about how to recognize a puppy farm seller.

With knowledge of this vital socialization learning stage, you can see why it's important that the first few weeks of your dog's life are happy and secure if they are going to be a completely confident adult dog.

Juvenile Learning

The juvenile learning period takes the puppy up to an adolescent, which for the Mini Aussie usually begins at around ten months old.

As a juvenile, the Miniature Australian Shepherd is in the perfect place for extending its social world. They can still learn to fear things, and may even go through a period where they seem to be worried about circumstances that previously didn't bother them.

This is part of growing up, and it is up to you at this point to make sure that they learn not to be worried about these things, and to be confident and happy in new situations.

Fear Stages

When a puppy is between six and twelve months old they are still learning what to be scared of. It is important to remember here, that by offering sympathy to any scared dog, we easily reinforce the fear.

If you respond to your dogs fear then it will become convinced that their worries are founded.

The idea when dealing with fear behavior is not to allow the dog to become overwhelmed, and at the same time for you to act in a matter of fact manner. Watch for signs of stress (described later), and if your dog is very worried, increase the distance between them and the stimulus if you can.

At this stage in their learning, a fear can easily be imprinted into their mind forever, so it is vital that you act confidently and allow them to overcome the fear without actually acknowledging it with a sympathetic reaction.

If a dog sees that its owner is unconcerned, then they will highly likely to be more confident in the situation during that time and in the future.

The Puppy Mill and Backyard Breeder

Thankfully the Mini Aussie is not currently at the top of the list for ruthless breeders, although other herding dogs are. As a dog breed gains in popularity, so do the amount of breeders that want to profit from them.

Therefore it is important that you are aware of the risks.

1. The first and most obvious problem is puppy farming. The puppy farmer can see two dogs of a much-desired breed, as a great investment. By buying a male and female, and having a litter every time the girl comes into season, the puppy farmer stands to make a lot of money.
2. Secondly the puppy farmer, or backyard breeder, avoids paying out too much during the process. So the bloodline of the dogs is suspect, health problems are usual, and the welfare of the puppy is often very poor.
3. Then the puppy farmer often keeps puppy parents in sad conditions. Sometimes litters are bred continually in a shed or large barn with numerous breeding adults.
4. Finally, when originating from this kind of breeder, a puppy will have no social contact until it arrives with you, and will probably have learnt to be afraid of people, because as we know, those first few weeks are crucial.

So how do you recognize the unscrupulous dog breeder?

There are a few things you can do in order to avoid buying a farmed puppy:

- Beware of anyone who wants to meet you with a puppy.

- Be suspicious of anyone who is happy to hand a dog over with no questions asked.

- Be suspicious of any seller that doesn't allow you to meet the dog's parents or see its environment. You can be certain that this type of breeder has secrets and they may not be very pleasant.

- Steer clear of pet store puppies as most are from puppy farms. Good breeders will not allow their dogs the distress of being sold from a pet store.

- Do not buy a puppy from classifieds or pet sites unless the breeder meets the specific standards laid out in the next chapter.

Another risk to be aware of is the classified sale. When looking for a Mini Aussie you will be able to find adverts online.

These adverts will be accompanied by pretty pictures of tiny dogs dressed up and are often Photoshopped. They will also be very helpful, offering to deliver you an Aussie puppy in return for advance payment. They often emphasize the words 'Mini' or 'tiny'.

Please don't entertain this type of advert. Often, and thankfully, the actual puppies don't exist, but the advertisers will be more than happy to take your money and vanish.

Find an Ethical Breeder

A good and ethical breeder of the Miniature Aussie will stand out from the more financially driven type of dog breeder. It is important that you learn to recognize a great breeder when looking for your new dog.

It is vital to begin the relationship with your new puppy by making sure you bring home a well-bred and properly socialized puppy or older dog. There are many people who call themselves dog breeders, but sadly only a small fraction of these are exceptional at the role.

The good breeder will have the welfare of every single puppy in mind and check carefully why you like the Mini Aussie. This is because they really care about where their puppies go.

There are generally less breeders of the smaller Aussie than other, more common dog breeds. However, the list of Mini Aussie breeders is growing along with the popularity of this dog.

The first thing a good dog breeder will do, as you approach them about a puppy, is to ask about your personal circumstances. They will probably ask for the following information;

- The type of home that you offer.
- Whether you have any other pets.
- Whether you have children.
- Why you want an Australian Shepherd and a Mini in particular.
- How much research you have carried out on the breed.
- How you intend to look after the puppy.

The mother will be whelped (give birth and raise her litter) indoors and as part of the family. Each mother will not be bred from more than a handful of times in their lifetime, and never more than once a year.

The breeder will be able to show you the puppies in a home environment, with their Mother and littermates.

Each puppy will be vet checked and at least first vaccinated before they are allowed to leave. The puppy will not be allowed to leave its Mom until it is at least six weeks old, usually eight. This is because there are important lessons for a puppy to learn from its mother in that first few weeks, as discussed earlier.

The breeder will want to be certain that you are educated in puppy care, that you have researched the breed, and that you know the potential risks.

When you visit the website of a great and dedicated breeder it may also appear full of rules and very strict. Remember though, it is only because they care, and the same attitude will ensure that they have bred only puppies of the finest health.

When you contact an ethical breeder they may even ask you to join a waiting list for a puppy. They will also offer to take the puppy back at any time, if you have to give them up for some reason.

By doing a thorough job you will find the whole experience, from finding a potential dog breeder, to choosing your puppy, very rewarding.

Many breeders also become long-term family friends. You have something very special in common after all, because you both want the very best for your dog.

The Older Dog

If a puppy is not for you, and not everyone wants the youngest dog possible, then why not consider offering a home to an older Mini Aussie?

Whether you look for a rescued Mini Australian Shepherd, or are taking one from a friend or breeder, there are often older dogs looking for homes.

In some cases, with herding breeds, a new family cannot cope with the energy levels of the dog as it grows. As a result of such unexpected needs and intelligence, plus the need for mental and physical stimulation, the Mini Aussie can often find itself in rescue or bundled off back to a breeder after only a few months.

Many dogs at this point have learned bad habits, although they can easily be reformed when they get the right and suitable amount of exercise in a more suitable home.

A Mini Aussie goes through adolescence at a few months old. Then they will begin to mature after that. This breed of dog is generally a mature dog quite early on, particularly when their needs are met.

If you are thinking that an older dog may be for you, take a good look at their history if possible to ensure that they will fit into your lifestyle, and that you are able to meet their needs.

The Mini Australian Shepherd as a breed will usually live a long and healthy life. They are robust and have a lot of stamina, so even if you decide to take home a dog at middle age, you can be sure that they have many years of hiking left in them.

Then of course there is the unwanted elderly dog. To be homeless in their twilight years is a very sad situation for any dog to find itself in.

If you can find a small place in your heart, and home for a greying muzzle and slightly blurry-eyed dog then do, for you may be their only chance. You will certainly not regret it, for this breed is no trouble in later years. They just want a bed, a bowl, and someone to call their own.

Rescue a Mini Australian Shepherd

Can you find a Mini Aussie in rescue?

Yes you can. Due to their busy natures and complex needs for stimulation, these little dogs are certainly at risk of being given up as they reach adolescence or even adulthood.

The adoption of rescue dogs is becoming more widespread, and easier. With social networking, and the broad base of Internet access, unwanted dogs are reaching new audiences. It is becoming increasingly popular for people to travel miles to meet a needy dog.

The Mini Aussie does occasionally end up in rescue, although not as frequently as a standard Aussie.

If you rescue a Mini Australian Shepherd you will not regret it. There is something special in a rescued dogs eyes. When we have a dog-sized space freed up in our home, we always rescue, and the choice has always been rewarding.

To find a local rescue that specializes in the Mini Aussie, it is worth first contacting a national rescue. They will then point you in the direction of your nearest breed-specific rescue. We will also supply information at the end of this book.

All-breed rescues should be able to help, although they do have waiting lists for some breeds and the Mini Aussie is still quite an unusual breed of dog.

A great rescue center will only rehome an Aussie when they have had full vaccinations and parasite treatment, a health check, a behavior assessment, and only then to a vetted home.

Shelters and dog pounds often regularly pass unwanted dogs over to rescue for assessment and rehoming. This is ideal as the dog is seen and tested in a domestic situation, and does not have to live in kennels whilst looking for a home.

If you are thinking of getting a new dog, please do not overlook the rescued and unwanted Aussies. Unwanted dogs have only been let down by humans, and in the right home this little dog will flourish.

If you rescue a dog you will be freeing up their space for another needy soul, so you will have saved two lives, which makes you a very special person indeed!

Male Mini Aussie, Female Mini Aussie and Neutering

The choice between a male or female dog is completely up to you. Generally people have their own preference. The differences between the behaviors of the sexes are pretty minimal. The physical differences are as follows.

The Male Aussie

For a male dog, as he grows up he will begin to mark his home and territory by lifting his leg.

Marking is a behavior that involves peeing on things. It can develop easily in a dog that is timid of nature. This is because a worried dog spreads his scent, in this way, to diffuse tension and feel secure.

With a generally highly-strung nature and a tendency to lean towards anxious behaviors, this little herding breed may feel the need to urinate to settle its fears.

This can become a habit that is difficult to overcome, and neutering is usually a way to combat the behavior. It is important to speak to your vet about timing, because neutering can also trap the marking behavior if carried out at the wrong time.

Another thing to speak to your vet about is whether neutering could adversely affect the behavior of your dog. Some very nervous dogs can become even more worried after the procedure.

An unneutered male may try to escape, as his thought processes are purely focused on trying to find a female. Without the additional hormones of an unneutered dog, the urge to wander is usually greatly diminished.

He may even mount and make love to anything, from legs, dogs, cushions, and all else that he sees fit for his advances if he is this way inclined.

An unneutered dog can become an unwilling target for other dogs too. Despite his behavior the little Aussie who has not been neutered can be attacked by other males purely because of his scent.

Neutering for a male dog is a simple operation. It consists of sedation and removal of the testicles, this also takes away all of the extra hormones that can make life as a domestic dog difficult.

Dependent on your geographical area the operation can cost an average of between US$80-150 (£70-150 or €50-140).

Many charities offer low cost neutering if necessary.

The Female Aussie

A female dog can get pregnant only when she is in season. During this time she will bleed from her vulva, and if you are part of an agility/flyball/training club she will certainly disrupt sessions.

The female season lasts for two weeks, and can occur between two and four times a year. You will notice it quickly because her vulva swells up and bleeds constantly.

Neutering for a female dog involves removal of the reproductive organs to prevent her coming into season at all. Life with a neutered female is a lot easier than dealing with messy seasons and unplanned, or even phantom pregnancies.

As a general rule, the female dog's behavior rarely changes when she is neutered. The operation will also prevent cancer and other problems in her reproductive areas later in life.

The cost for a female neutering operation will range between US$100-$200 (£100-180 or €80-200) dependent on size and area.

As with the male dog, many charities will help subsidize the operation if financial help is needed.

Should You Get Two Dogs Together?

Whether you decide to have one or two Mini Australian Shepherd dogs is completely up to you. There are pros and cons to either choice.

There is however some basic things that will happen if you bring two puppies home from the same litter.

With two dogs bought into the home as puppies at the same time, whether they are siblings or not, the pair will bond with each other before they bond with you.

This is great if you have a busy lifestyle because they will always have each other for company. Each will have a live-in playmate.

The problem with this is that it is very difficult to train two dogs together. If the pair is bonded as well, it can be hard to part them for training.

That said, and if you are new to dog ownership, you may be better getting one dog for a few months. Then when the first dog is trained and good behavior is established, you can introduce a second, younger dog. That way your first dog will help to train the puppy.

Dogs are group animals and deserve some canine friends. This is equally true whether your Mini Aussie gets safe playtime with other people's dogs or their very own canine companion at home.

Kids and Other Pets – Includes Introductions

The Mini Aussie can live happily with children and even other pets. It is important that they are introduced carefully to everyone in the home right at the beginning.

Too much stimulation can cause problems, particularly when a dog is new to a home and probably already confused.

As quite a gentle dog, the Mini Aussie will live happily with cats and other small furry pets, but must be supervised to keep everyone safe. They will also quite enjoy a canine companion.

Canine Introductions

When you introduce a new dog into the house where an existing dog already lives, it is vital that you begin the introductions outside of the home. Take both dogs for a walk together first of all. Keep both of them on the leash and allow them to say hello. Then if possible allow them to play off their leashes together, before bringing them home.

It can be tempting to interfere with dogs as they get used to living together. It can also be tempting to ensure that the existing dog does not feel pushed out. Just be careful with this, the best thing you can do is carry on as normal and allow the new dog to tag along with your normal routine.

Cats and other Little Furries

When introducing to cats and small animals, it's important to keep the new dog under control and give the existing pet an escape route if they need one.

Cats are quite good at getting up high and observing a new dog down below until they feel safe. You must allow this to happen and allow the cat to get used to the dog in his or her own time.

No dog should ever be allowed direct and unsupervised access to small furries, as any dog can have an instinctive reaction, and the risk is simply not worth it.

Dogs and Kids

When you bring a new dog home to a house with children, it's important that you teach the children to respect the space of the dog. The Mini Aussie will struggle if it is crowded and cornered.

Dogs should not be expected to cope with children poking and harassing them. Each dog is an individual in their own right, and by allowing children to fiddle, you will be taking a risk with both the dog and the child's well-being.

That said, kids and dogs can have the best relationship in the world. They seem to understand each other and the Mini Aussie will undoubtedly appreciate the constant play and ball throwing that the child will happily supply.

In many ways every child should have a dog, and every dog should have their very own human child. The two seem to belong together.

Initially, and as your dog grows, the kids may be excited and desperate to pass it around. It is therefore vital that you remember any dog in a new home will need its own space. The Mini Aussie, along with any other dog, if stressed, scared or hurt, may snap.

It is vital that children learn about canine communication and behavior, alongside body language, in the same way as everyone else in the family when you bring a dog home.

What it Costs to Buy a Mini Australian Shepherd

The cost of a Mini Aussie varies greatly depending on breeder type, geographical area and whether you bring home a puppy or a rescue dog.

A good breeder that has carefully matched parent dogs, who has raised the puppies with love and socialization, will charge US$800-1200 (£500-800 or €800-1200) for a perfect Aussie puppy.

The general rule with dog breeders is that cheaper puppies have usually been cheaper to breed and raise, thus corners have been cut. This will certainly show in the health and behavior of a dog as it grows.

If you are rescuing a Mini Aussie then most rescue centers charge a set fee, which can range from US$50-200 (£50-150 or €50-200)

The rescue center will usually greatly lower the fee for adopting an elderly or less healthy dog. They are generally pleased to get the older Mini Aussie into a loving home, so will absorb the cost of caring so far.

Donations into rescue go towards caring for other dogs, and also covering the cost of any veterinary treatment, feeding, transport and general care of the dog whilst they were in rescue care. A rescue donation often does not cover the complete cost of rescuing the animal, it just helps.

Section 3 – Your New Dog

When it's time to bring your new dog home you will undoubtedly be excited. You will want to get everything right and it's important that you know as much as possible about taking care of your new friend.

So in this section we are going to cover basic canine care, health and well-being of the Miniature Australian Shepherd, alongside preparation for its arrival, which is of course is the most exciting part of all!

Puppy Preparation

When all the research and waiting is done, the next step is getting your home ready. It is not too different preparing for a puppy than it is to making a home childproof.

We will talk about puppy preparation here, because the littlest dogs often get into the most trouble. If you are bringing home an older dog it is equally important to ensure the following, and that they stay safe.

- All harmful substances need to be out of reach or locked away.
- The puppy should not be allowed near the stairs because a fall could damage them greatly. It is certainly worth investing in baby gates if you cannot shut the stairs behind a door.
- Chocolate is poisonous to dogs, so is cocoa mulch on your flower borders, so be aware that neither of these should be within your puppy's reach.
- A puppy will go through teething, much as a human baby does, and your dog will need safe and specific teething aids to chew. These can be recommended from your vet or bought at a local pet store.
- Be careful with rubbish and waste food, because your Aussie may believe that everything is fair game for putting in its mouth, and look out for poisonous plants in your garden too.
- If you have a pond or pool, block access to your new dog indefinitely. Take a wander around your home and garden and try to see through the eyes of a youngster, where everything is interesting. Then simply make everything that may be interesting, yet hazardous, unobtainable.

Your dog will probably still fiddle with something but your job is to make sure their choice is no danger to them.

The Dog Focused Shopper

Here are some essentials that you will need for your dog.

- A bed that they can call his or her own and retire to when they want, or their behavior prompts some time out.
- A crate, if you plan to use one. The crate is a great idea for any dog.
- Dog clothing if your home is chilly, particularly if you are bringing home a puppy, because it will be used to the warmth from its mother and siblings. It will be better to invest in a couple of long lasting fleecy jumpers than keep buying cheaper ones.
- A nice selection of dog toys for playtime, interaction and teething if necessary.
- A selection of grooming tools.

All about Dog Food

It is easy to get drawn into the marketing and advertising of commercial dog foods.

Each meal promises the healthiest, tastiest and most perfect dinner that a dog can ever encounter. Every pet food producer states that their food is the best and that by feeding your dog with their culinary delights, you are providing the best possible care to your canine friend.

Like all other clever marketing campaigns, pet food manufactures embellish and rely on their carefully planned advertising, gaining our trust.

In this area we are going to introduce you to some truths on commercial dog food. Some of this you may find uncomfortable, yet it is true and for your sake and the sake of your dog it is better to be informed.

So let us take a good look at commercial dog food. First of all I would like you to think of it in the way you would with human food, is it full of preservatives and colorings.

There is little doubt the preservatives, additives and colorings in dog food will change the health and behavior of your dog.

I read recently, in an article by a worldwide established canine behaviorist, that whenever a dog owner reports canine behavior problems and asks for help, the first question that he always asks is 'what does the dog eat?'.

This is because additives to food, which are wholly common in commercial pet food, will have an effect on your dog similar to E numbers on a child.

That wonderfully colored bowl of kibble, with its reds, oranges and greens may look and smell perfect to you, but to your dog it is a mood-changing helping of chemicals that they could really do without.

In the same article, the same behaviorist, informed the reader that a lot of potential canine behavior consultations were never carried out, simply because the dog owner trialed a change of their dog's diet instead. The problem behavior greatly diminished and the dog became an altogether easier addition to the household.

The lesson with this is not to look at the behavior without looking also at the ingredients.

Hypoallergenic dog food is free of fillers, additives, colorings, wheat and preservatives. It is often labeled as premium dog food in today's market. These are high quality foods, certainly in comparison to most of the supermarket brands.

What Dog Food Manufacturers Don't Advertise

Pet foods are usually a mixture of meat, byproduct, fillers and wheat or cereal. This sounds quite straightforward right? The only questionable ingredient is the filler, right?

Fillers offer a cheap way to bulk out the dog food and to fill up the dog. This ingredient really has no part in the nutritional value of the food. Common fillers are feathers, animal hair, citrus pulps and other vegetables.

Common byproducts are crushed hooves, intestines and even undeveloped eggs.

Wheat has a growing reputation as an irritant for dogs. In surveys carried out over the last few years, wheat ingestion has been linked to skin problems, allergies, depression and even seizures in dogs.

Meat is the main ingredient of dog food most of the time. However, 'meat' is a loose term and it is vital to read between the lines on each ingredient list. The meat used in pet foods can vary from human grade meat through to road kill, and some areas even recycle the bodies of euthanized, unwanted cats and dogs from shelters into pet food.

As you can see it is vital to take a lot of care when reading the ingredients on the food that your dog is going to eat.

Weaning

Weaning gradually onto a new food is important. Doing this correctly will give your dog the best chance of keeping a settled stomach during the change process.

It's a simple process where over a few days you gradually mix the current and future food, giving your dog's stomach a chance to adjust.

Home Made Dog Food

You may even find that homemade food works perfectly for you. I make my own dog food every week on shopping day, and the dogs certainly prefer it.

But how do you know what meats and vegetables to buy? In regards to meats, your decision should be based on what your Mini Australian Shepherd would naturally eat in the wild. As they are small sheep dogs, then they would only be able to kill lightweight animals ranging from chickens to sheep. Therefore in the supermarket you would choose white up to the lighter colored meats.

In regards to vegetables, again you must look at how they eat in the wild. After killing an animal, one of the first things they eat is the intestine, which is full of partially digested grass. Now seeing as partially digested grass isn't available in supermarkets, you need to feed your dog partially cooked vegetables such as broccoli and other greens. Partially cooking greens also prevent thyroid problems, such as hyperthyroidism.

With oven cooked meats, boiled rice, partially cooked veggies and sweet potatoes, added together and blended to whichever consistency you prefer, you can easily create a homemade dog's dinner that will last in the fridge for a few days.

There are certain nutrients that they will need to ensure they will grow properly, but if you use meat and introduce a lot of leafy green veg, you can create a nice array of recipes to keep your pet healthy and happy.

The following is a list of food to include in your dog's diet:

- Organic meats
- Oily fish
- Rice
- Leafy green veg
- Pulses – lentils and chickpeas.
- Sweet potato
- Carrots
- Apple (not seeds)

Foods to avoid

The following foods will harm your dog. There are mixed opinions of feeding bones yet, whether cooked or raw, small parts of a bone can get stuck in the dogs intestine with serious or even fatal consequences.

As a dog owner that almost lost a little dog in this exact circumstance, I have added them to the list, to make you aware of the risk of feeding bones to your dog. The list is as follows:

- <u>Animal Products:</u> Bones, bacon & bacon fat
- Chocolate
- Nuts
- Onions
- Raisins and some grapes
- Dairy produce - dogs are generally lactose intolerant

Feeding Tips

Your dog should always have unlimited access to fresh and clean drinking water. I have heard advice being given, in the past, to take water away either for toilet training or as an odd kind of dog training. Please always allow your dog access to drinking water - it is one of their basic rights, and one of your responsibilities as their guardian.

A good breeder, or rescue center will advise you on the type of food the dog currently eats, and how many times a day they are being fed at the moment. They may even send you away with an amount of their current food to help wean your dog onto what you would prefer to feed them.

Dry food or kibble is probably the easiest to prepare, with a squirt of warm water and a tasty morsel to start off the eating process. There are many dry food types from numerous manufacturers. Remember to check the ingredients and read between the lines.

Tinned food is often highly processed meat that contains water, flavorings, and can be quite salty. Therefore a dog will need a lot of tinned food if this is their main diet due to the low nutrition value, and even fed with biscuits this can equate to expensive feeding.

The cheaper foods can seem better value, however the higher quality food is fed in smaller quantities due to the nutritional value being better concentrated, therefore the saving can deceive.

You may try your dog on different foods before settling on one type. Be careful if changing food and always follow the weaning process described in this chapter.

Dependent on the feeding route you decide to go down, it will be a good idea to budget an approximate US$40 (£30 or €40) to feed your dog each week. This is a generous estimate and includes training treats.

Essential Physical Exercise

A healthy adult Mini Australian Shepherd will need plenty of exercise.

As a working breed with huge amounts of intelligence and stamina, they need to be using up the energy they were born with.

This fit little Aussie will keep up with the exercise levels in most active homes. It will be happy to hike for many miles, and take great pleasure in sports that take advantage of its focus and energy.

At the very least a regular and daily run is necessary to prevent problems related to excess mental and physical energy. Unused energy within the highly intelligent and reactive Mini Australian Shepherd can lead to:

- Destructive behavior
- Barking
- Stealing
- Aggression
- Mental instability
- Depression
- Weight gain
- Hyperactivity
- Self-mutilation
- Shadow and light chasing

It is surprising how many people ask for advice on the behavior of their dog without first assessing whether the dog has enough exercise. A dog that is chasing its tail is saying that it needs to use up its energy.

The dog that jumps to its feet at the moment you move, wants to go outside and run around.

Vaccinations

Your puppy will also need vaccinations before you take it out into areas with other dogs. Its immune system is still developing and vaccinations will prevent the contraction of a potentially fatal disease.

A puppy will also need their exercise levels built up gradually until it is fully grown. Remember that its bones are still growing, and too much exercise may cause developmental problems.

On your puppy's initial health check and vaccination appointment, it is important to speak to your vet about any disease risk in your particular area. Your vet will also check their joints and tell you how much distance your puppy should walk in its first few months.

Make the most of this time because in a year or so your Mini Australian Shepherd will have more energy than you can imagine.

They will want to walk whether the sun is shining, rain is pouring down, or it's up to its shoulders in snow, because being active is one of their biggest pleasures.

Essential Social Fulfillment

Socialization is vitally important for your Mini Aussie. If a puppy is socialized properly and responsibly, then it will become a mentally healthy and confident adult dog.

As a herding breed, the Mini Australian Shepherd can tend to be a little reactive and even nippy towards dogs that invade their space. Remember they are bred to work alone in plenty of space, and not to be directly approached by all manner of dogs, people or other animals.

To sum up socialization in a sentence would be 'to ensure that a puppy encounters every possible experience, in a positive manner, in order to become confident and happy in all situations'.

If you have a puppy or even an older Mini Australian Shepherd, it is your job to introduce them to everything that you possibly can, in a responsible and positive manner. It is also vital that you read their body language to see how well they are coping. The idea is not to overwhelm them.

The list is long but here are some ideas of areas for social introductions with your dog:

- Travel: Herding dogs can develop problems in the car. With their genetic herder 'eye', the quick movement of other cars or the scenery through the window can overly excite them, leading to a very noisy trip.
- Children
- Cats
- Dogs
- Walking beside moving vehicles and bicycles
- Pushchairs
- People
- Farm animals

- Thunder and fireworks (this is important, and you can play a CD in the background at home to allow your pet to learn that these sounds are normal). We will cover sound sensitivity in the last area of the book.
- Crowds

With plenty of positive social introductions, most puppies will become happy, unconcerned older dogs. The key is to keep everything relaxed and not to allow your puppy to become worried. To have a positive effect on your puppy you can ask people and children to be gentle with your young dog, and introduce them slowly to positive and friendly older dogs.

Speak to your vet about whether it is safe in your local area to carry your puppy, out and about, before their vaccination course is finished. The few weeks between vaccinations can be used as a crucial learning time, albeit under your jacket, if your vet deems the outings to be low risk.

Soon you will be able to walk your puppy, but be careful, as it is small and fairly delicate. A fumbling Labrador or other big dog could easily hurt them, so be alert to the risks.

Remember also that it is still in an intense learning stage for those first few weeks with you, and as it grows, keep them safe and ensure that the dogs they interact with are kind. The area on canine body language, in this book, is a good place to visit, in order to learn about the body language between dogs, before you go walking.

Dogs will learn good manners from other dogs better than they can learn from any human. They need canine contact as much as we humans need to have other people around.

The owner that plans to do agility or other sports with their Mini Aussie will greatly benefit from taking them to puppy classes and even into the sporting environment as soon as possible. This will get them quickly used to the noise, smells, and an abundance of other dogs.

Housebreaking

One of the most questioned topics on dog training is that of housebreaking. When you bring home a puppy from a good breeder, the process of toilet training will already have begun.

One thing to remember when potty training a puppy or dog of any age, is that there will certainly be accidents.

There is a lot of conflicting advice on the subject, which can cause problems. By handling the initial process badly at the beginning, a well-meaning new dog owner can actually cause long term housebreaking problems.

Train – Don't Punish

An old fashioned view of efficient house training is to rub the dog's nose in its mess. Never do that. It may also be natural to tell your dog off if it does have an accident indoors. Don't do that either. Neither of these actions will help and they are very unfair on the dog.

Like everything else your puppy needs to know what you want from them, and it is up to you to demonstrate. Never punish your puppy if they have an accident in the home. They simply haven't learned yet where they should go to "perform".

1. Offer your puppy plenty of opportunity to toilet outside. Go outside every hour at the beginning to show that they are not alone out there. Gradually reduce the frequency that you take them out and eventually your puppy will trot outside and go whilst you wait by the door.
2. Observe your dog throughout and then when they do toilet outdoors, reward the action with plenty of praise and a game or treat. Puppy training pads, placed by the door, will help them go towards the door and be less messy if they can't hold it in.

3. A young dog wants to please you. They like the result that your pleasure provides, which is praise and a reward. Therefore by showing your dog that you are over the moon with their action of toileting outdoors, you will trigger something in them that makes them want to repeat the action.

It won't happen overnight, but by repeating this over a few days you will be using positive reinforcement to toilet train your puppy.

You can also use a crate when you need to leave your puppy on its own inside. They are more likely to hold it in when in the crate, because it will be less willing to soil its sleeping area. Just don't be away too long, or else an accident will inevitably happen.

The Older Aussie

When an older dog toilets indoors, there may be other reasons for their behavior. They could be stressed or worried. Dogs that suffer from separation anxiety often toilet indoors and if your male dog is adult and unneutered, their hormones could be dictating their behavior.

If you rescue an older dog, then expect a couple of accidents in the beginning, even if it is already house trained. Remember it is feeling a lot of stress and upheaval, and their toileting behavior will eventually settle down the more relaxed in the new environment it becomes.

A Collar, Harness and Walking on a Leash

If you are the owner of a new puppy, you will need to teach your Mini Aussie to walk on a leash so that you can take them out for walks in safety.

This is not a natural behavior for any dog, and such restriction should always be introduced with positive kindness.

A harness is usually a better choice for smaller dogs to prevent trachea problems developing from pulling when wearing a collar. If you prefer a collar, then ensure it is wide and comfortable.

Start with a collar or harness, the right size for your dog and lightweight, and put it on your dog in the house.

In the beginning a puppy may think it can't possibly move whilst wearing the walking attire. They may stand completely still and look really miserable, but don't worry about that, they will get used to wearing it; your job now is to distract it.

Do something interesting with your Aussie. When helping a dog to be comfy in their new collar or harness you can play with a toy, do some basic training, give them their dinner, or even throw tiny treats for them to gather up. When your dog forgets it has the walking wear on, simply take it off and put it aside.

After doing this a few times and when your dog is relaxed, it is time to add a lightweight leash to the established attire. Don't hold the leash, just attach it and let it trail behind as you play in the same manner as you always do with your Aussie. Only when your dog is relaxed at this stage, is it time to move onto the next step.

Soon your dog will forget that they are wearing anything at all, and then you can start to hold the end of the leash. When your dog is relaxed with you holding the leash, you are ready to go for a walk.

Off-leash walking with a Mini Aussie puppy is actually quite easy. They are highly unlikely to run away. Start in a safe enclosed area where you know they are safe. If you take along some tasty treats and call your dog back regularly then they will soon learn great recall.

All dogs need the opportunity for a free run, and when as a puppy, your Aussie will happily toddle along with you.

As it grows, it is vital that your Mini Australian Shepherd learns to come back when called. The breed usually responds really well to whistle training and general recall practice, particularly when treats or a tennis ball are involved.

A Dog Crate

The dog crate is something that more and more dog owners are embracing. They help with training, toileting, and even sound phobias. The crate is far removed from the restrictive cage that it was once seen as.

I highly recommend that you crate train your dog, and also do it in a positive manner, whatever its age.

Dog crates come in varying sizes and types. There is the chrome or metal crate, and also a portable canvas crate.

Bear in mind that metal is generally indestructible and inescapable. The determined Aussie will be able to get out of a canvas one with perseverance - leaving you with a ripped and useless crate.

Crate Expectations

The main thing about introducing your Mini Aussie to their new crate, is to keep the introduction highly rewarding and positive.

If any dog is pushed into a crate and shut in straightaway it will be understandably worried. Such an approach may even cause a long-term fear. However if you make the crate a positive experience, then your dog will accept it gratefully as part of their personal space area.

Excellent crate training follows a positive process. This is described below:

- Put the crate initially in an area of the home where the dog can see you.
- Place a really comfy bed and blanket into it.
- Put some toys into the crate, maybe even a Kong or other interactive toy and allow your dog to lie inside, whilst they empty the tasty treat, but leave the door open so that they don't feel trapped.
- Feed your dog in the crate with the door open.

- Throw treats in one by one and allow your puppy to go in and fetch them.
- When your Aussie is happy in the crate, you can begin to close the door.
- Crate training will help with toilet training, because a dog will rarely toilet in their own sleeping area if they can help it. If your puppy can wander across the room and pee, then go back to its own clean bed; it may see no point in holding itself. The crate simply compacts its living situation to help prevent this behavior developing.
- It will also help a dog who is worried by noises, because a blanket can be put over the crate, to provide a secure den for the worried Aussie. This is particularly important for this breed, as they are prone to sound sensitivity.
- Never use the crate for isolation after unwanted behavior. If the safe place has a negative association, the dog will never relax in it.

An interactive toy given regularly inside will ensure that your dog sees their crate, not only as their own space, but also as a place where positive things happen to them.

Home Alone

The Mini Aussie is particularly susceptible to separation anxiety and the breed will probably be unhappy if it is left home alone a lot. They need to be with people and busy to be a happy dog; this is what its genes dictate.

The best thing that you can do is teach your dog that alone time need not be stressful or worrying for them. This will help it to cope better on those days when it has to be left for a while.

Whether you will be leaving your Aussie alone regularly, or not at all, it's very important for them to get used to being left for reasonable periods of time. You should do this from the day you bring your puppy home.

If you have a puppy, and never need to leave it alone, but at a year old your circumstances change, you will probably have a stressed little dog on your hands.

With separation anxiety, prevention is always better than cure, so get your Aussie into the habit of spending some relaxing time alone from day one. This is doubly important with this breed because they can easily become overly attached.

Start with a few minutes at a time and just leave the room, then the house, after giving your dog a special treat or toy. Wait outside and watch your dog if you can. If it makes a noise and looks worried just wait for them to settle before you re-enter the room. This way the dog won't think it has actually called you back.

Then gradually build up to going out for an hour or so. If you have a young puppy, they will soon learn that you leaving them alone for short periods of time is just a normal part of their everyday life.

Grooming Your Mini

The Mini Aussie is a dog that will shed its coat regularly, so will not need a clip or even to visit a groomer at all unless you specifically want them to.

To groom at home is easy. You will need a shedding comb for their undercoat and a wide toothed comb for the top layer of hair.

The Aussie is double coated in order to stay warm when working in cold weather. The top layer is meant to ward away rain and the underneath provides warmth and insulation.

With a double coat, the underneath layer can become loose, particularly when the dog is shedding and can get stuck in the top layer of hair if not groomed away. This trapped hair will result in a tufty coat and can be avoided with the use of a shedding comb specific for double-coated breeds.

Start at your dog's head and work through its coat to remove any tangles before they become knots. If your dog expects pulled hair, they will not want to be groomed for long. Stop regularly and give them a tiny treat, this will keep it happy and relaxed.

Bath time

Bathing a Mini is usually pretty easy. Baby shampoo or a very gentle adult shampoo is fine, or special dog shampoo. The Aussie really only needs bathing when they are really mucky. A good brush a couple of times a week should keep your dog relatively clean and its coat healthy.

A Pampering Session

Some dog owners like to use a dog groomer to keep their pet clean and smelling fresh.

A good professional groomer should cut your dog's nails, clean their teeth, and pluck excess hair from within their ears. If you do choose a groomer, like everything else, check their customer reviews and experience with the breed.

For a bath and comb the groomer costs will be approximately US$50-60 (£40 or €40-€80).

Handling and Health Checks

The more a dog is handled as a puppy the happier they will be.

Handling your Aussie every day is more than just keeping it clean and health checked. It will help you to bond and prevent future problems. Handling can be carried out whilst grooming your Aussie or just when you think of it during the day. Check the dog's feet, ears, eyes, and teeth.

If you are starting with a very young puppy, then daily handling should be easy, as it will not have built up any resistance. An Aussie who is as young as three months old and has not been handled can become a problem.

If you have bought home an older Aussie who has not been regularly handled from a young age, they may struggle initially during grooming and handling sessions.

The struggling will be due to worry on the dog's part, and needs to be handled gently and carefully to avoid confrontation or stress.

Positive Handling

Keep the actions very relaxed and build the dog up gently with lots for reward. By doing this regularly you can prepare yourself and your dog for when you need to administer medications, cut nails and check teeth.

To combat any reluctance you can bring nice treats into the session and take things slowly. Touching different areas of their body at your dog's pace.

Putting time and patience into grooming and handling will prepare your dog for any veterinary treatment that they may need. This will help them stay as relaxed as possible during veterinary surgery visits and if having treatment administered at home.

Regular health checking is essential and you can do this at home yourself. Here is what to look for:

Eyes

Remember that the little Aussie can develop eye problems very quickly, so it is vital to take good care and pay extra attention to its eyes.

Your dog's eyes should be clear and bright without excessive discharge, apart from that leftover from sleeping. Older dog's eyes may show signs of bluing or becoming cloudy. This could be a sign of cataracts, and if you are worried then it is worth speaking to your vet.

Ears

Your dog's ears should be frequently checked. Look for a dark discharge or regular scratching, as this can be the sign of infection. Affected ears can also have a stronger smell than usual.

Dogs that have a lot of hair growing inside the ear can struggle with infection, as the hair can prevent normal healthy wax leaving the ear area. This can be a problem in longer haired Aussies. Professional groomers often remove excess hair from the ears when grooming a dog.

Ear mites can become a problem if your dog comes in contact with an infected animal. Too small to be seen by the naked eye, a bad ear mite infestation can cause the dog a lot of unrest and distress. Both infections and ear mites can be diagnosed and treated easily with drops, antibiotics, or both, prescribed by your vet.

Teeth

Check your dog's teeth regularly to avoid tartar build up. Toothpaste specifically for dogs is available from your vet or pet shop, often meat tasting, which your dog will welcome. If you cannot manage to brush their teeth, some toothpastes work by being squeezed over food. Look for enzymatic canine toothpaste for the best result.

By taking extra care of your dog's teeth early on, you may be able to prevent problems later in their life.

Pet food providers offer chews and treats that have added teeth cleaning benefits within them. These are an option, but if you choose to feed them it's worth monitoring their effectiveness by checking your dog's teeth regularly.

If the Mini Aussie will eat a raw carrot it will naturally clean its teeth. They may not be keen on carrots but some dogs love them and they are a super healthy snack.

Anal Glands

Anal glands can become impacted or infected. If they do, then the anus area, where the two tiny glands are located, will appear swollen and possibly look like two lumps or boils have appeared.

Your dog may be licking its anal area. Scooting across grass or your carpet will also show that irritation in the tender area is present. If you are suspicious of such infection, then it's important to take your dog to the vet.

Nails

Dog's nails also need to be kept short to avoid pain on walking. Regular exercise on either concrete or other abrasive areas will wear the nails down naturally. Exclusively grass walked dogs and older, less exercised dogs are likely to need their nails cutting more frequently.

You can buy nail clippers, but one thing to know is that a dogs quick grows right into its nail, which is fine for clear toenails because you can see it, but not so useful for black ones. If you choose to cut your dog's nails at home then always just nip off the end, otherwise you could hurt them and they will never let you near their feet again.

Coat

If the coat becomes dry at all with dandruff, then it's either one of two things that could be the cause.

1) Washed with hot water, which is more than the actual body temperature of the dog. This will actually kill the layer of skin causing dandruff, because dogs can't sweat through their skin – they sweat through their paws and through their mouth.

2) Not enough of the essential fatty acids in their diet. They get the fatty acids from such foods as partially cooked vegetables (especially the greens), and some need more than others, so vary their diet accordingly. This is not canola oil or vegetable oil, but rather the Omega Oils, particularly Omega 3. Dry food is normally high in Omega 6, which is not good for them and tends to lead to obesity, the same as humans.

Skin

If your dog is biting at its feet, scratching its underbelly, or for non-castrated males scratching its testicles, this is often due to a contact problem commonly caused by the high use of disinfectants used within its environment.

If your dog is scratching all over, and there are no fleas present, this is due to dry skin, caused by either warmer than body temperature washes, or a lack of essential fatty acids in its diet, particularly Omega 3 (must be high quality fish oils). It could also be caused by ingestion problems due to additives or dyes in the dog's food.

On rare occasions an allergy to meat can also cause skin problems, however, as we mentioned previously, if you stick with lighter meats such as chicken and lamb, that your dog would normally eat in the wild, you shouldn't have any problems.

Signs of illness

The thing that every Mini Aussie owner dreads is illness. It is difficult to see our little friends poorly or in pain. Sometimes it will happen and here are some things to look out for.

If you catch most illnesses, and treat them early enough, healing will come quickly.

Behavior changes are often the first sign that a dog is not well. Tiredness, excessive drinking, and uncharacteristic refusal of food are all concerns that should be taken seriously.

An owner that is in tune with their Aussie will know instinctively when something is wrong with their dog. Unfortunately our dogs cannot explain in our language why they are off color, so we must try our best to understand, and if necessary provide the ailing dog with expert medical attention.

Vomiting

Dogs can vomit as they choose. With one episode of vomiting from an otherwise healthy dog, it is worth just keeping an eye on them to ensure it does not happen again.

A dog will often regurgitate grass, and normally this is nothing to worry about. Eating grass may sooth a sickly stomach and grass contains a natural painkiller so all the dog is doing is taking an option to feel better.

One episode of eating grass is not normally a cause for concern. Springtime may encourage grass eating as some dogs tend to like the fresh green shoots.

Prolonged episodes or violent vomiting should be seen by the vet. This is extremely important particularly if the dog has recently had a bone or tends to eat objects. This type of sickness could be caused by a blockage in the digestive system and could be life threatening.

It is paramount that on contacting the vet you explain the possibility of a blockage by foreign object, because action will need to be taken immediately to help your dog.

Any sign of blood in the vomit should also be seen by the vet.

Diarrhea

Diarrhea is a symptom that could go away on its own within a couple of days or be pointing to something more serious. If your dog has mild diarrhea or loose bowel movements but otherwise looks healthy, it is worth keeping an eye on its health for a day or so before becoming too worried.

Diarrhea could be caused by a food type that they are just not used to, or your dog could just be a little off color. In this case it may be worth not feeding your dog for a day to allow their digestive system to recover and then offering something bland such as chicken and rice on the second day.

Consistent and persistent diarrhea is a worry. Blood in the urine or excrement is also a concern. If your dog is not managing to keep any food or liquid in their body because of the diarrhea, then it may become dehydrated and have to go into the vets for intravenous fluid treatment. Further investigation will be needed for prolonged episodes to identify the cause of the condition.

Checking for dehydration

If you gently pinch the back of your dog's neck, lifting up an area of the skin, it should spring back into place quickly. The skin of a dehydrated dog will not do this and will stay in place for longer. By doing this technique you can roughly check whether you dog is becoming dehydrated.

Two or three days of diarrhea are enough to cause sufficient concern and the vet should be contacted.

Kennel Cough

Kennel cough is a distressing disease for both dog and owner. It is highly contagious and any animal suspected of having kennel cough should be isolated from other dogs as much as possible to prevent the spreading of infection.

Dogs that have been living in a kennel environment or around a lot of other dogs are at risk of contracting this infection, and many dog pounds and rescue centers have to deal with it regularly.

An infected dog can carry the cough for months despite consistent treatment from the vet, and the harsh hacking cough coupled with phlegm patches around the home, will drive even the most patient and loving owner to distraction.

The Kennel cough vaccination is offered by vets, however unless your dog is going into a high-risk environment, you may prefer not to vaccinate against it.

Eyes and Ears

An eye or ear problem should be seen by the vet.

Don't be tempted to buy over the counter medicine for an obvious eye or ear problem, unless advised by your vet. Home treatment can end up in learning a painful and expensive lesson for both you and your Aussie.

In a puppy farm environment there are lots of dogs, and should a serious illness occur, it will pass through the litters quickly. There are many horror stories of puppies being bought from poor breeding situations and becoming so ill that they could not be saved.

This is partly why a puppy should at least have proof of its first vaccination and veterinary checks when you collect it from the breeder.

Be Parasite Aware

There are a number of parasites to look out for when you are taking care of a dog. Each of the following can be easily treated with a veterinary approved medication.

Some pet stores sell insecticides that are not veterinary approved, I suggest that you steer clear of this treatment type as they can cause severe allergic reaction in a dog.

Herding dogs in particular have a high risk of chemical allergy and this certainly includes the Mini Aussie.

Fleas

Fleas live in the dog's coat and bite its flesh to suck its blood. They run around and can jump a long way. A flea infestation will be apparent by little black grit like substances in the Aussie coat – flea dirt, and if wetted it turns red. The dog will be itchy and you might even find a flea on you or the furniture.

Ticks

Ticks are tiny before they get onto a dog. They bury their head under their skin and suck blood. They can become the size of a grape when full and simply drop off again when satisfied. Ticks will feed from animals and humans. They live in wooded areas and high cattle areas.

A veterinary flea treatment will protect your Aussie from both of these parasites.

Worms

Fleas and worms often go hand in hand, so to speak. Which is why when flea treatment is given, worming should occur too. Puppy worming is different to adult dog worming, as a puppy will need a specific wormer.

Heartworm

Heartworm is becoming an increasingly worrying risk, as dogs travel more and more with their owners.

The heartworm is a parasite that can kill the dog. The worms are picked up by eating slugs and snails and if untreated will cause organ failure in a dog. Many vets that have experienced the effects of heartworm in their geographical area, now offer preventative treatment.

Mange

Mange is caused by a tiny mite that lives on, and in the skin of a dog. It is often seen in unwanted or street dogs because it eventually causes complete hair loss.

If left untreated, mange mites attack the immune system of a dog leaving them highly susceptible to illness. Eventually a severe case of mange, built up over a long time will affect their major organs.

Mange is another parasite that is treatable with veterinary attention, and that is also preventable with the suitable medicine.

Find a Great Vet

Choosing the right veterinary practice and a good veterinary surgeon is one of the main things for a dog owner to do. It has to be someone that you trust and are comfortable with.

Ask around friends and family to see which vet they prefer. Word of mouth from other dog owners is a great idea. Such research will provide you with far more information than simply choosing a vet based on location or his or her own personal advertising.

You will get a good feeling about the vet that you want to see each time your dog is poorly. Do not be shy either about changing vets until you get the right one. Veterinary surgeons are only people after all, and some we get on with, whilst others we don't.

Remember that your regular vet will be around whilst your Aussie is ill, which will be a stressful time, so it is important that you trust and like them.

When meeting a new vet it is worth watching carefully how they are with your dog. Observe how the dog reacts to the vet's touch, and a good vet will explain to you what they are doing and what they are looking for, every step of the way.

When you have chosen your vet you will use them for:

- Vaccinations
- Boosters
- Flea and worming treatments
- Weight management

All of the above are essential health maintenance treatments to keep your Aussie happy, healthy and parasite free.

A good veterinary surgeon will explain the difference in the treatments that they stock and help you to make the right choice for your own dog.

The Consultation

Dogs all react differently to a veterinary surgery visit. Many Aussies love the stimulation of a full waiting room and the lavish attention of a consultation.

Some dogs will fear the vet visit, particularly if they have received a lot of treatment or don't enjoy being handled. Some owners find taking their dog to the vet stressful, and the dog will pick up on this and mirror the stress.

If you have a dog that is extremely fearful of the vet and you can afford it, then it is worth having the dog treated at home.

To desensitize a dog you can go into the surgery regularly without seeing the vet. Many people weigh their dogs in the waiting room once a week then leave again.

A good surgery will encourage this as it should reduce the dogs fear and also give you, and them, an opportunity to watch the dog's weight.

Costs will obviously vary depending where you are. Most good vets now also offer a lifetime service where you can pay a monthly or yearly premium, which covers vaccinations, boosters and all necessary parasite treatments. Taking an offer like that can save you some money in the long run.

Micro chipping, Vaccinations and Insurance

Micro chipping is a great idea. It is the act of inserting a tiny chip under your dog's skin then registering their home and your contact details on a national database.

Many vets and rescue centers check, with a specially designed scanner, for a microchip, the moment they receive a lost dog.

The act of Micro chipping is gradually becoming a legal requirement on an international basis and goes hand in hand with responsible dog ownership.

Vaccinations

The main illnesses that can be fatal to any puppy are vaccinated against. These are canine parvovirus, distemper, hepatitis, and in certain areas leptospirosis. But always check with your vet first. Any good breeder will vaccinate before allowing the puppy to leave, and will often have already paid for any initial second vaccination that is needed. A booster will be given every 12-18 months to ensure that the dog stays protected.

If your puppy's mother had been vaccinated before she had her litter, her maternal antibodies (from her colostrum) can normally remain in her puppies up to about 15-16 weeks of age. Therefore if you vaccinate your puppy between 6-14 weeks of age, you will only be giving a small boost to their immune system. This is because there is already a really high amount of antibodies provided from its mother in the puppy's system, causing the antibodies from the vaccination injection to be neutralized almost immediately.

By 15-16 weeks of age, the mother's antibodies will start to disappear; therefore it is a good idea to give them another boost during this time. This immunity boost will then last until 12-18 months of age. Follow this up with boosters annually for the next 2-

3 years, then every 3-4 years after that due to the high levels of antibodies built-up.

You may need to give vaccination boosters every 12-18 months for the rest of its life, if as your puppy grows into an adult dog, it has been completely isolated and not let outside or allowed to socialize with other animals. This is due to the dog not picking up any antigens from its environment, that are needed to create antibodies for its immune system, the same as people.

Insurance

Insurance is a personal choice. The average regular insurance premium will cost US$50-60 (£30-60 or €50-80) per month. If your dog is a working dog, such as search and rescue, this must be mentioned to the insurance company.

When choosing insurance it is important to read between the lines. Some companies will not always renew cover after a certain age. Look for a company that offers lifetime cover despite any long term illness.

Travelling with Your Mini Aussie

Your dog will travel easily in any form of transport if introduced early enough.

Travel Sickness and Stress

Travel sickness can be a problem with some dogs. This constant worry of being sick can lead them to experience travel stress. Symptoms of travel stress are drooling, panting, barking and vomiting.

The best thing to try if your Aussie is sick or stressed in the car, is a herbal travel sickness remedy; your vet may be able to help with the best one in your area.

Bach Rescue remedy or Adaptil are also good for a stressed dog. The first is a herbal flower remedy, and the second a spray form of a copy of female dog hormones, similar to the hormones a mother dog produces around her puppies. They work to calm the anxious dog.

Pets Travel Scheme

With the pets travel scheme replacing the old quarantine requirements, your Mini Aussie can even travel between certain countries if they had had full vaccinations. This includes a rabies vaccination and blood test to confirm immunity to the disease, and proof of specific worm treatments.

You will find more information on the scheme in the links at the back of this book.

Travel Safety

Safety when you travel with your Mini Aussie is paramount. Whether you are only going a few miles or a few hundred, it is vital that your dog is safe.

It is important that your dog will be as safe as you can make them in the event of an accident. Whether you do this via a canine seatbelt attached around your dog's body, or a crate in the vehicle is up to you.

A Word on Heat

Heat is a serious subject when travelling with a dog. Any dog can die in a hot car. It takes less than ten minutes, even with the windows open and when it doesn't seem very hot at all.

Dogs cool their bodies down by panting. Only if the air around them is cooler than their body temperature, is this effective. In a hot car, the air around them will not allow this cooling, and the dog will quickly suffer from heat exhaustion.

So if you are traveling with your Aussie, please never take the risk of leaving them in a hot car, not even for a few minutes. It's really not worth it.

This is also worth remembering if your dog is left in a car on a ferry journey, and even when you are walking together on hot days.

Walking in the midday sun is also highly unadvisable. When the weather is so hot that the dog gets no chance to cool down, it is highly susceptible to heat stroke. The Mini Aussie is double coated as we know, therefore he can overheat very quickly.

Section 4 – All About Dog Training

The Miniature Australian Shepherd is a dog that will respond perfectly to dog training. In actual fact they are usually happier during dog training sessions than at any other time.

Their trainability is so high that the Aussie will learn very quickly and be obsessed with being busy. This is exactly why this type of dog continuously brings back a tennis ball or similar toy.

Dog training can be confusing, particularly with all the advice we encounter.

We are told to be the boss, to show dominance, to embrace reward based training, and a mixture of so many methods that it's easy to become overwhelmed.

During this section of the book we are going to talk about dog training in general, the best way to teach your dog something new and how to understand the learning process of the Mini Aussie, in order to train it perfectly and with kindness.

Dog Training Terms – What They Mean

Here are a few dog training terms to look out for, what they mean, and whether they will suit your Mini Aussie Shepherd.

Dominance

When you are looking into dog training, either in your local area or online, you will come across the theory of dominance. It may be worded differently. It could be called pack leadership, be the boss or even be the alpha.

This training method is based on the premise that every dog is a wolf underneath. It was designed following a study on a captive wolf pack a long time ago.

The original wolf pack, because they were fenced in and forced together, behaved unnaturally. There was friction between them and certain members of the group were forced into roles which they did not suit.

This caused problems. Not unlike a group of people pushed together with no escape. At the time of observation scientists came to the conclusion that there was a constant struggle for leadership, or the alpha role, within the group.

Sadly the behavior of the wolves was labeled as natural. Following that a whole new dog training method was based upon the inaccurate assessment of a struggle for leadership.

This training method includes things like physical punishment, eating before the dog, and standing in their bed. One of the most worrying is something called an 'alpha roll' where the dog is physically rolled over onto its back. This is meant to mimic the actions of a stronger wolf and put the dog in its place. It is a dangerous and unnecessary act.

Please stay away from this type of training, for your sake and the sake of your Aussie.

Within the last few years dog training has taken a turn for the better. With the introduction of more accurate scientific research, we have a much better idea of how our dogs learn. This is where positive dog training comes in.

Good dog training will be a positive experience for both you and your Aussie Shepherd.

Positive Reinforcement

Positive dog training is based on a method that we call reinforcement. There are two types of reinforcement: positive and negative.

Positive reinforcement is the act of rewarding your dog for a behavior that you would like them to repeat.

Positive dog training makes the most of reward, by timing it well. Good dog trainers always encourage the dog to carry out nice behavior in order to earn a reward.

Negative Reinforcement

Negative reinforcement is the act of taking something away when a dog ceases to carry out an unwanted behavior. For instance, if my dog was barking and I pulled a bit of his hair until the barking stopped, I have used negative reinforcement.

I would be teaching my dog that for as long as he continues to bark I will continue to pull his hair and thus hurt him. Negative reinforcement is quite old fashioned and similar in many ways to punishment. This can consist of hitting or threatening a dog.

Punishment

Punishment is not a method that is used during positive dog training. The reason is simple; punishment will not work in the long term.

To punish a dog after a behavior has been carried out will not stop the behavior being repeated, it is too late for that. Every single time a behavior is carried out, the dog is forming a habit. Whatever happens afterwards, whether the dog is hurt or scared, is completely unlinked in their mind to their behavior that it has just been displayed.

Punishment will only produce a scared dog that feels like it cannot trust its owner or trainer.

The act of teaching a dog to do something else instead of the unwanted behavior is much better dog training, because it actually teaches the dog a better way.

It may seem a little complicated now but by the end of the next few pages you will have a good grasp of how positive dog training works.

Positive Reinforcement in 3 Easy Stages

Positive reinforcement is a method that will revolutionize your dog training experiences. It is so simple that you can apply the three stages given here to anything that you want your dog to learn and they will work.

Within this book we want to give you the skills to train your Mini Aussie, from puppyhood, to do anything you would like him to. We believe this is a far better method than offering step-by-step instructions for specific commands.

If you apply the following steps, your dog will certainly learn. Of this I have no doubt.

Step One - Motivate

Find out what it is that motivates your Mini Aussie. Most herders are obsessed with a tennis ball. This obsession almost seems genetic. During this step try a few different reward types and see which one your dog gets wide-eyed and excited about.

Step Two – Refuse/ Reinforce

As a highly intelligent and inventive breed, when motivated, the Mini Aussie will begin to display specific behaviors. They do this in order to get you to hand over whatever motivates them.

At this point it is your job to refuse to hand over the reward for anything other than the desired result.

Then you wait until they carry out the behavior, then quickly mark it with praise or a click (explained soon), then hand over the reward. As you hand over the reward say the command that you would like this particular behavior to be called.

The act of marking a behavior then handing over the reward is called reinforcement. This reinforcement and ultimate reward will be how your clever little dog learns to repeat the behavior.

Step Three – Encourage if Needed

Some of the more complex behaviors may be taught by the method of lure and capture.

This is the act of gently encouraging a certain behavior before capturing it with reinforcement. It just makes things quicker.

For instance, if you want your dog to look you in the face and focus, but it won't get the idea, you can bring the reward down behind your head the capture the look their eyes follow it. When they eventually look in your face, you can reinforce the look quickly and efficiently.

So there you have it, dog training in three easy steps. Why not practice with the following: sit, down, focus, paw touch, roll-over.

With the three steps above and the highly intelligent Mini Aussie, the sky really is your limit!

The Puppy Class

Puppy classes are great. Your veterinary surgery will be able to tell you when and where your local puppy class is held. Many practices actually run their own puppy classes in order to help new owners socialize their young dogs.

If you decide to take your Mini Australian Shepherd puppy to a puppy class, it is important to remember, that puppies of all sizes are going to be there. Because your own puppy will be very small you must take care that it does not get hurt.

Some puppy classes actually cater to specific sizes of dog, and whilst this is a good idea in some ways, it is still important to ensure that your puppy still gets a lot of positive experiences around dogs of all sizes. This socialization will help them to grow up into a well-rounded and confident adult dog.

When choosing a puppy class look for one that is run by an experienced, positive, and reward based dog trainer. That means the class must be punishment free, happy, and confidence building for your dog.

Remember that each and every learning experience, from the moment you bring your puppy home, will create the adult dog that your Mini Aussie will become.

Dog Training at Home

Many puppy classes only last a few sessions.

Some can then point you in the direction of an equally beneficial older dog training class. If you want to carry on with the training of your Aussie, then more classes may be just the thing for you.

The first thing to do before deciding what to do next with your rapidly growing puppy, is to decide what you want from them. In other words, how do you want your dog to behave?

Some dog owners enjoy a cheeky little dog and allow some pushy behavior. Other dog owners, however, lose control of their dog's behavior, which can end up causing serious problems.

It is all very well having a dog that is a bit cheeky, it can even become amusing, but if that behavior becomes a problem then something must be done. The dog must learn appropriate behavior for both theirs and your sake.

So, do you want an Aussie who will jump through hoops? A dog who knows a repertoire of a thousand impressive tricks? Or are you happy with a dog that will curl up on your lap when asked to and come back when called?

It is important to know this before moving on with your dog training. After all, if you don't know how you would like them to act, how is your dog going to know?

Clicker Training

Clicker training is positive reinforcement at its very best. The clicker is used to capture and reinforce any behavior which you would like your Aussie to repeat.

The first stage of clicker training is to teach your dog that the sound means a treat is on the way.

Treats should be really small for clicker training - just enough for a taste, so that training is not interrupted by lots of chewing. A taste will motivate your dog better than a mouthful.

Think of how wonderful one square of forbidden chocolate is to you, then how different you would feel about it if you ate the whole block. This is the result we are aiming for with clicker treats.

Teaching a dog that the click is a positive sound, is called 'tuning in'. You can do this by spending a few minutes pressing the clicker once, then handing over a tiny treat. Then repeat the same session five or six times, and before you know it your Aussie will expect a treat whenever it hears the click.

You can test this by waiting for your Aussie to be looking elsewhere and then you press the clicker. If your dog looks straight at you then they are tuned in to the sound.

Now, from this point on, when you press the clicker, you will reinforce anything your dog is doing at the time they hear the sound.

The only rules of clicker training are:

Always hand over a treat every time you press the clicker, otherwise your dog will not respond to the sound. The treat gives the click power, and even if you click the wrong thing, you must always give your dog their treat.

Never use your click to call your dog back. This is because when your dog hears the click as they are running away, the sound will reinforce the behavior of running away.

For an Aussie who is sound sensitive and does not like the click, you still have options. You can wrap the clicker into a towel or cloth to muffle the sound. Some pet stores also sell clicker bugs, which are a tiny version of a clicker and great for sensitive ears.

The other option is to say the word 'click' at the point where you would normally press the clicker. You would need to say it in the same way every time, and even tune in your dog the same, as if you are using a clicker. By doing things this way, your timing may not be as sharp, but it will still work.

High Energy Activity for the Breed

The reason that the Australian Shepherd and the Mini Aussie are so popular in dog sports is that they are so good at them.

Super speedy, quick-witted and flawlessly intelligent makes this dog breed a fantastic candidate for any type of advanced training. The Aussie is also so energetic and has endless stamina, which is exactly why they are becoming a highly popular agility dog.

Here are some ideas of canine sports that your little Aussie will love. Be warned, many are highly addictive and to join a team will probably take over your life.

Agility

Agility consists of teaching a dog to negotiate a series of obstacles in as short a time as possible, and to perfection.

Competition agility is competitive indeed. Many owners and their dogs spend every weekend at competitions during the season. The dogs love the challenge and the winning team is the dog that can clear the course the quickest and pick up the least faults.

Flyball

Flyball is great fun and increasing in popularity. It consists of a team of dogs and their owners, a box that throws out a tennis ball, plus a set of hurdles. Flyball is a relay game of speed. Each dog negotiates the hurdles, grabs the ball and returns to its handler. Then the next does the same until all the team has ran. Two teams run side by side and the winning team is the one that finishes first.

The hurdles of a flyball team are only as high as the shortest dog. If there is a 'Mini' in the team then the hurdles are lowered.

Cani X

Cani X is a running sport. The dog is attached to its owner via a waist belt and the two run together through trails and courses. The winner is the fastest to finish. There are many events during the Cani X season, run primarily in the cooler months.

Search and Rescue

The Mini Aussie is a perfect candidate to become a search and rescue dog. They are bred for air-scenting and stamina. Many organizations are happy to recruit a search and rescue team for the role, which is usually voluntary.

Search and Rescue work is all encompassing; you can be called out at any time of the day or night to look for a missing child or hikers lost on the hillside.

This vocation really is a lifestyle choice but, as someone with search experience, I can only say it is a wonderful thing to get involved in.

Obedience and Canine Freestyle

Competitive obedience and canine freestyle are also fantastic fun. Whether you choose obedience, which can be a little serious, or decide to teach your dog to dance with you for fun, the Aussie will love the experience.

Any activity where they are constantly learning and perfecting a skill, will keep your Mini Aussie happy and full of enthusiasm.

Training the Older Dog

You can teach an 'old dog new tricks', and in actual fact you should.

Learning is great for an older dogs mind. It can even chase away depression and the onset of canine dementia. Teaching a dog of any age new things will be a fantastic relationship boost between you, and you will both enjoy it immensely.

If your Mini Aussie is in recuperation or struggles with its joints, do not despair. A dog does not need to be highly active to learn and enjoy training. There are plenty of things that any dog can learn without moving too far from their bed, or the sofa.

For instance, why not teach your dog to put their paw over their nose. It is a very cute trick. Or to growl on command, yawn or even sneeze on command.

This is the beauty of reinforcement training. You simply show your Aussie a reward and capture the behavior you would like them to repeat with your click, before you hand over the reward.

Your older Aussie does not need to jump through hoops to gain the benefit of learning.

Recall Training

It is a good idea to teach recall (coming back when called) to any dog of any age, including the Mini Aussie, although they rarely develop problems.

Nevertheless, here is how to train any dog to come back - in seven easy stages:

1. Begin training at home and then gradually move on to training outdoors. Begin by showing your dog a treat and stepping back away from them, then saying their name. As your dog comes to you, tell them that they are a good dog and give them a treat.
2. A helper would be a good idea at this point because they can hold the dog whilst you show the treat and walk away, then they can release it as you say the dog's name.
3. Gently increase the distance between you both as your dog responds well to the recall.

4. Then repeat the entire process again at the park. Start small again then increase the distance as your Aussie manages to come when called.
5. You can run away and hide when you become confident that your dog will work to find you.
6. If your dog is ignoring your call, then don't chase him unless you are worried about its safety. Instead make it want to come to you by offering something irresistible.
7. The trick with good recall is to always be the most interesting thing at the park, so if you have to carry a squeaky toy, use a high pitched voice or even run away singing your dog's name then do so. All are much better options than a lost dog.

You can use your clicker in a recall context but only when your Aussie is already en route to you. You want to reward their return when they are already returning and not before. Remember the click is very specific. The sound will always encourage the dog to repeat exactly what they are doing at the time.

Section 5 - Behavior and Canine Understanding

One of the biggest misconceptions about dog training and behavior is that only the elite can understand dogs.

This is why so many people can set themselves up as unregulated dog trainers and behaviorists. It is also why people can call themselves dog whisperer's and earn a substantial living by giving out, often inaccurate, advice.

I am here to tell you that you can understand your dog. To do so is pretty simple unless your Aussie has serious behavior issues. In this case it is important to go to someone who knows the science behind dog behavior, a qualified expert.

General dog behavior is pretty straightforward. If your Aussie insists on behaving in a certain way it is often for one of the reasons detailed below;

1. He is scared
2. He finds the behavior rewarding
3. You are inadvertently reinforcing the act

Each of the reasons above can be linked to either of the others. The first thing for you to do is work out which of the reasons is paramount for the particular behavior of your dog. The next thing to do is change the circumstance to change the behavior.

We will go into more detail about this in the next few pages.

Understand Linked Behavior

An important thing to understand about your new puppy, and any dog, is that their behavior will reflect yours. It will also reflect anyone else in the home, and the behavior of any other pet you may have. This is because, once your new puppy has left its Mother, your Aussie will begin to learn from the other people and animals in its environment.

So if you keep this in mind it will be easier for you to work out why your dog is acting in a certain way. If you respond in a way that is positive in your dog's mind, then the puppy will repeat the behavior.

Attention

Dogs love attention, and this is a very important thing to remember. They don't care if the attention is delivered in a positive form or a negative form. So if you are telling your Aussie that it is a good puppy, in a happy voice, or informing it sternly that it must be quiet, they don't care. Either way it has your attention.

All attention is rewarding and by realizing this you can look at how your own behavior affects the actions of your dog.

Try it for a while. Each time your dog does something which you would like them to stop doing, ignore them, then when they carry out nicer behavior, reward with attention. You will soon see the behavior of your puppy begin to improve.

Attention Shapes Behavior

When you become aware that your Aussie is behaving in a certain way, to get your attention, you can start to change how you react in everyday situations.

When shaping a dog or puppy's behavior, a good rule to live by is the act of ignoring unhelpful behavior and rewarding helpful behavior.

This is easier said than done, I hear you say, and yes it is very difficult to ignore a cheeky dog initially, but it does become a habit quite quickly. When your dog learns that you are not going to react to a specific behavior, in the way you have done previously, it will stop bothering.

An Example

So let's look at one common problem behavior and how we can, as owners, be teaching our dogs to repeat it regularly.

A Mini Aussie can easily learn to demand bark for attention. Barking is an Aussie trait and this is why a bark can easily become the 'go to' behavior of the Aussie.

Here is an example of both responses and how they affect your dog;

The dog barks and you look towards it, and then call it to you. Next time it wants attention what do you think it will do? The bark worked, so why not use it again.

Now in another scenario, the Aussie barks and no one looks towards them. It is like the noise never happened, so it gives up and lies down. When they are quiet you call your dog over and give them some praise and attention. Now it has learned that barking does nothing, yet settling gets some positive attention.

If you apply this reasoning to daily life with your puppy, then you will find it becomes second nature to shape your Aussie and their general behavior to perfection.

General Body Language

This is one of the most important parts of this book! Everyone that lives with a dog should learn basic canine body language and communication signals.

You may even already be aware of certain aspects of canine body language. The posture, tail, and facial expressions of a dog, all display its mood and reaction to stimulus. A dog will use their face, tail, and posture, and even become vocal to let us know what it wants.

The same body language would often be unnecessary when it is communicating with a social member of its own species. Humans, however, naturally expect dogs to understand us, our gestures and our words.

To be fair to them, the domestic dog has worked hard to understand us a lot of the time. They teach themselves by the process of elimination and consequence, what certain things mean. We owe them the same courtesy.

The Dog's Face

Facial expressions in a dog are a big clue to how a dog is feeling. Here is what they mean.

- Licking lips or nose – Nervous, worried
- Yawning – A calming signal detailed below
- Panting without heat or exercise – Anxious/stressed
- Focus of eyes on a subject – tense and may issue a challenge
- Ears pricked - interested
- Ears back – worried, or if right back excited and maybe expecting a treat
- Eyes whites showing – tense, look at the facial muscles because if they are tense too this dog may snap.
- Squinty and relaxed facial muscles – happy

Muzzle pulled back teeth showing – This dog is warning you, they will bite if pushed. Interestingly, some dog's show teeth on greeting. They offer a submissive grin, which is offered naturally at first and often reinforced as a smile. So if this facial position is offered but accompanied with other submissive and squirmy body language, then it is often the dog's own unique greeting.

The Dog's Tail

Tail position is another way that the dog communicates.

- A natural tail carriage which varies between dogs – a happy and relaxed dog.
- Tail tucked underneath back legs – worried.
- Tail held higher than normal – the dog is aroused, this often happens when meeting a new dog.
- Tail pushed straight upwards or over back with hair bristling at base – Aggressive or challenging.

The Chatty Dog

Some dogs are more vocal than others by nature. Some even learn to bark at the point in their lives where they find out it benefits them. Others rarely bark at all.

- A dog's bark varies dependent on its pitch, tone and frequency.
- A single yelp – shock, fear or pain
- A continuous yelp – distress or prolonged fear/shock/pain
- One high pitched bark – excitement, and a few of these are used for attention or food demand barking
- Three or four medium pitch barks – Something is happening, everyone be alert
- A tirade of continual medium to high pitched barking – danger

Howling is often used by dogs in an attempt to spread their bark over a longer distance. As wolves howl to communicate at distance, so do dogs.

Dogs tend to whine when they are unhappy. Boredom, separation anxiety or loneliness can create a whining dog. The canine is asking for something and by looking at its general circumstances you should be able to tell what it is.

Another time that whining occurs is excitement, such as when you get the leash out or fill up the food bowl.

Growling for a Reason

Growling is another thing altogether. A dog uses its growl as an attempt to warn and send something away. It is usually something or someone that it perceives as a threat to their situation, personal space or their belongings.

Growling is more progressive than barking because it starts low and deep in the throat. As the threat continues, the growl gets louder until it becomes deep, and the dogs lip and muzzle can wrinkle back. If the growl is not heeded at that point the dog may snap and continue to growl. The next step for them would be a freeze and then a bite because it has given fair warning.

The Aussie in general is not much of a growler. It is more likely to show its teeth and then snap if pushed to its limits.

The idea of great communication with a dog is not to ever hear it growl by always setting up situations which it can cope with. Some dogs have learned to growl, or even bite, at any stimulus and in this case will need behavior modification.

Artificial breeding and body language in dogs

This section does not apply to your Mini Aussie per se. I wanted to add it in order for you to see how your own dog may see other dogs that it meets.

You may wonder why it acted in a certain way towards that muscular boxer dog or showed some fear towards the generally stiff looking chow breed.

Often this is because artificial breeding has taken away the ability, of some dog breeds, to communicate to their full potential.

Thankfully tail docking is gradually becoming illegal for appearance reasons, as it takes away a big part of the communication toolbox of a dog.

Dogs that are bred to have a tail curling over the back can give the appearance of a posture that they have not purposely adopted.

Breeding for a muscular appearance can give the dog an appearance of an enhanced or even aggressive posture.

Dogs that are bred to be long coated lose the ability to use hackles in order to communicate. If facial hair is long then the facial expression can even be obscured.

Canine Communication

We already know that a puppy is born with a certain amount of ability to communicate. After the neonatal phase when it simply wants to eat and sleep, the puppy, as it begins to interact with others of its litter, learns the benefit of a wagging tail to diffuse tension.

This ability is limited, because if the puppy is taken away from other dogs during the imprinting stages of their learning, then it may never really communicate properly with dogs again. So from this we can be certain that much of a dog's communication techniques are learned from others of its species.

This becomes obvious when a dog has not been allowed to communicate with other dogs as it has grown up. It has missed out on learning manners and social etiquette. Then when it meets another dog, they either misread or completely miss all of its signals, resulting in a bad experience for everyone involved. This is what often happens during a dogfight. This is also usually why a dog on a tight leash bounces and barks towards another dog.

Communication signals between dogs are very subtle, and if untrained, the human eye will often miss them altogether. Dogs will use calming signals when meeting another dog to show that they are no threat. They will also use the same calming signals if worried by a person or situation that they cannot control or escape from.

Interestingly we humans often use the same signals when interacting with each other - but not always for the same reasons.

Calming signals

Calming signals are obvious to an approaching, well-socialized dog, and will be to you when you know what to look for. Mild calming signals will often be displayed in any circumstance that a dog feels stress on a low level.

Each or any of the combinations below may be displayed.

Mild Calming Signals

- Yawning
- Licking their lips
- Glancing away or staring elsewhere
- Excessive blinking
- Scratching themselves
- Raising a paw
- Dipping their head slightly
- Sneezing or snuffling
- Wandering away
- Sniffing the ground
- Whining – a generally vocal dog will whine if slightly stressed.

Appeasement

If a dog wants to show an approaching canine, other animal or person that they are no threat, then they will often behave like a puppy. The behavior includes holding its body low, wriggling, licking the lips of another dog, rolling over to show its belly and even urinating.

What this dog is saying is that it is not a threat; it just wants to be friends and would love to play.

This behavior is called appeasement. By acting like a puppy and licking around the face as if to a Mother, the wriggling dog is actually saying that it is at the complete disposal of the other dog.

Other appeasement signals are displayed for the same reason. The dog that jumps up or rolls over and urinates, is trying to send out the same message.

These signals, if they work for the dog, will disappear quickly. After all they were there to show the other canine that it was no threat. If the dynamics between the two change, then the signals of appeasement may return.

Aggression or Reactivity

Hopefully you will never see aggression from your Mini Aussie. If they are well socialized and cared for, plus its communication attempts adhered to, the dog needs never become aggressive at all.

If you do have problems with aggressive behavior from your dog it is important never to engineer confrontation. If you are worried about coping, then it is time to call someone in to help you to understand it and cope with it.

Aggressive behavior can develop in any dog when it feels it has no choice. Unfortunately then it can become a habit. The more often aggression works for a dog, the quicker an aggressive response will be displayed.

Aggression can arise from the following situations;

- Fear – The dog is frightened of someone or something
- Pain – The dog is hurt or in pain
- Possession – The dog is guarding a resource

How Does Aggression Become a Bite?

The following steps show each step of behavior that the dog will display before resorting to biting.

1. Focus. The dog will lock their eyes onto the subject of its aggression.
2. Calming signals are displayed. These consist of glancing away, yawning or licking its lips. The dog will attempt to calm down, and communicate this to whatever, or whomever worries them.
3. Next the dog will then change its posture, shift its bodyweight, their hackles may raise and they may growl.
4. If growling doesn't work the dog will show its teeth.

5. If flashing the teeth doesn't work they may snap at the air between your dog and the thing or person they are worried about.

6. Then the dog may freeze. This is a very brief act and consists of the dog going completely rigid, which is evidence of the dog making a decision to either fight or flee the threat. If they can't leave the situation, the dog is at severe risk of biting. This is because it feels like it has no choice - and to be fair, they have given a lot of warning.

People can often tell off a growling dog automatically when it is simply trying to communicate that they are unhappy. As a dog owner it is far more important to work out the reason for the growling, when it is a new behavior, than it is to stop it without knowing why it occurs.

Here is an example of the dog that growls when it is worried by the presence of a stranger.

If your dog growls when a stranger reaches out to touch it then that is usually because they are scared. Normally a person will be wise enough to back away from a growling dog, thus rewarding the hostile behavior by showing the worried Aussie that growling works.

To growl will remove the threat. Your dog is well within its rights to do this. It is up to you to protect them from that fear by asking people not to approach them directly. This request will prevent the fear and prevent the growling.

You can counteract the fear reaction by asking people to ignore the dog and just talk directly to you. You can then move on to asking strangers to drop small treats, then eventually to offer those treats directly to your dog. Depending on the intensity of the fear this could take months. Gradually your Aussie will stop seeing strangers as a threat.

An important thing to know is that the more competent at aggression a dog becomes, the quicker they will move to biting.

They could even miss out the other stages. This is because they may have learned that it is the only thing that works for it.

Fear Aggression

When a dog is fear aggressive it can show in many forms. Take a look at the body language chapter to see fear type behavior. It is important that the scared dog is never challenged and always given an escape route. It is vital that a careful and gentle modification program is put into place for this type of aggression.

Pain

Unusual and sudden aggression could be related to illness or pain. If your dog suddenly becomes aggressive for no apparent reason, or when it is touched or approached, then it is vital that you take them to the vets.

Guarding Resources

The dog that guards resources, and even the dog that doesn't, will benefit from being taught to swap resources. Toys are one of the Aussies favorite things, so make sure it has plenty to play with and swap them regularly.

If your dog guards food, then swap for something that it can't resist. If it growls over its food bowl, it is because they are scared that allowing someone to approach will mean the food goes away.

By adding a couple of extra food bowls at mealtimes, then putting food into each in turn then walking away, you will show the dog that an approach to a food bowl is a good, not bad thing.

It is vital to seek proper professional advice on an individual problem that you can't seem to make progress on.

Remember to look for a qualified behavior counselor and steer clear of anyone who talks too much about dominance. This approach can, often in the long term, make aggressive behavior worse.

Yapping

Yapping is certainly a behavior which the Aussie is capable of displaying, again and again. The little dog will soon learn that yapping gets attention, and to an Aussie, and most other dogs, attention is one of the most rewarding things you can give to them.

So if your dog is a barker and it is driving you nutty, take a look at your own behavior when they bark. Do you talk to it, pick it up, give it a treat or a toy or even its meal? Any of these things are teaching your Aussie to bark louder and more frequently.

Attention is seen as encouragement, by your dog, despite the words that you are using and even how the words are delivered.

So remember we said about rewarding the behavior which you would like your dog to repeat? In this case it is important to reward your Aussie when it is quiet. To do this, and this may sound odd, you need to teach your yapping dog to bark on command.

1. Begin with a clicker (or your word) and a treat, then withhold their treat whilst the dog tries to work out how they can get it from you.
2. If they jump up, take the treat further away. The dog will then try other behaviors.
3. Eventually they will make a sound. Whether it is a yap or even a whine it is important then to reward the sound. So capture the behavior, with a click, and hand over the reward.
4. Repeat this a few times and then add the command which you would like to use when you want your dog to bark. I use the word speak, but anything is fine.
5. If you repeat this entire session a few times over a couple of days, using the command every time, then your Aussie will begin to bark on command for a treat.

6. When you reach the stage above it is time to add the command which you will use to silence your dog. I use the word 'quiet'. Simply wait for a natural pause between barks, click the quiet behavior and use the command.

Finally practice alternating between asking your dog to bark then asking for silence, and you will soon be able to bring this training into your everyday life.

Herding, Lights and Shadows

Herding behavior and light or shadow chasing are behaviors usually, but not exclusively, shown by working breed and high-energy dogs.

Because your little Aussie is a herding breed things that may not affect others will catch their eye. Remember they were bred to bring flocks of sheep into order, notice the occasional lamb in the distance, and watch out for the quick movements of predators.

These behaviors usually occur within a dog that does not get enough suitable stimulation and exercise. Sometimes the behavior just becomes a habit and then escalates into an obsessive disorder.

Herding behavior

Herding behavior should never be encouraged. Do not allow children to run around whilst your dog is chasing them. The more excited it gets the more likely your little Aussie is to begin to herd.

It may even herd dogs if you take it to the park and could possibly even herd groups of people. If it begins to get over excited, it is vital that you put your dog on a leash until it settles down.

Shadow and Light Chasing

This behavior can become a real problem and even if your dog shows no sign of displaying it so far, it is important to watch out for it developing.

You can prepare your home for a dog to provide minimal opportunity for becoming obsessed with light. Be careful with ornaments and curtain types that throw gleaming patches of light onto the ground and walls. These could easily be enough to begin a problem in the Mini Aussie.

Exercise and Distract

If either of these problems begins to develop in your dog the most important thing to ask yourself is whether you are meeting their needs.

Is your Aussie getting enough training and exercise for a dog with its working drive?

If it is, then to prevent the habit from developing further, offer a distraction instead. If you suspect that your dog is paying attention, to the point where learning and obsession interrupt their behavior, then give them something else to do.

Stuffed toys, mental stimulation games or even a good run will take their mind off the intriguing lights or groups that they would like to organize.

Sound Sensitivity

The herding breeds are often sound sensitive.

When a dog is sensitive to sound, fireworks, thunder and shooting will upset them greatly. This is a difficult thing to experience and also for you, as the dog's owner, to witness.

Fireworks, in many places, are used for weeks at a time and freely available to buy in many stores. Around holiday periods and festivals they can ring through the air for long before and after the actual festival date, leaving sound sensitive dogs reeling in their wake.

Sound Related Stress Prevention

If you are bringing home an Aussie puppy one of the best things you can invest in is a sound socialization recording. This is usually a CD that plays the main sounds on a loop. This allows the puppy to get used to the noises, as they play quietly in the background, well before they flood its world.

A recording will even help the older, fearful dog, if it is played very low and in the background when it is otherwise relaxing. Look out for signs of stress, because the idea is to make the sound barely noticeable and gradually increase it, as they are able to relax around it.

The Stressed Dog

When your dog is stressed already then you can only deal with them in order to try to minimize it.

Rescue remedy, calming solutions from your vet, or Adaptil available online, may minimize the psychological trauma for the sound sensitive dog. Each dog is individual, so trial and error is a good way to decide what is best for your own little Aussie.

A Thundershirt is also a proven way to calm some dogs. The Thundershirt is a tight item of 'clothing' that the dog wears in stressful situations.

It works by wrapping the chest and torso of the dog and applying pressure enough to naturally calm the worries.

Another thing you can do during times of high noise is to provide your dog with somewhere to go away and hide. A crate or table with a thick blanket over it offers a 'cave of safety', which will give the dog a sense of security whilst they are worried.

You can play music loudly, close the curtains or put on a noisy movie. Remember never to sympathize. If you show sympathy or appear worried to an already scared dog then you are likely to reinforce the fear and make them even more worried.

The final thing to do when your dog is scared this way is to be extra secure. Many dogs can run away during firework season, because fear will replace rational thinking in the canine mind. So keep the doors closed, keep them on the leash if you go out, and make sure that your garden is extra safe.

Separation Anxiety

A dog that is left alone regularly, for short periods, from puppyhood will be at less risk of developing separation anxiety. This is because they learn that reasonable periods of alone time are normal.

Separation anxiety can take many forms;

- Destructive behavior
- Pacing
- Whining, barking and howling
- Defecating
- Self-harm

So if you have a new puppy, the best thing to do is begin leaving them for short periods as early as possible. If you are using a crate for your Aussie then you can pop them in there with a treat and a special toy whilst you go out of the room for a while.

When saying goodbye to your dog don't make a fuss about it. Simply hand over something nice and use a phrase such as 'won't be long'. If your Aussie thinks that you are worried then they will be worried too.

If your dog already has separation anxiety then you will benefit from going through the puppy stages too. Begin by introducing a nice toy. A Kong, or activity ball which you can stuff with something really tasty, will keep them occupied.

Then introduce a new bed or blanket. This is the bed that your dog will eventually relax on with their Kong whilst you are out.

Introduce a radio or leave the TV on for your dog when you go out. Dogs generally enjoy classical music.

Start by leaving the room for a few seconds then just build up to leaving the house. The idea is to get your dog relaxed when alone, but depending on the severity of its anxiety, this may take a while.

Calling in an Expert

When a behavior is established in the dog then a modification process will take place. This is a case of rewiring the dogs thought process into something more useful.

Dog training is unregulated. Unlike doctors, nurses, teachers and their assistants, the dog trainer is not required by law to pass an exam in order to practice the profession. So it is up to the dog owner to make sure that the training advice that they seek is not going to harm their dog or make their behavior worse.

If you are looking for specialist help with your own little Aussie, it is important to find a qualified behaviorist or trainer. Always check references and trust your instinct when you first meet someone.

A behavior modification program will start with a consultation where the expert observes your dog. They will work out why the behavior occurs, what is causing it to continue, and even in some ways how the dog is feeling.

The good behaviorist will often then go away for a couple of days before returning with a modification program specific to your dog.

The program will be kind, understanding and never hurt or frighten your dog. It will be explained carefully to you, and each step kept simple enough for the dog to cope with.

In a good behavior modification program there is never any confrontation between the expert, you as the dog owner and the dog. The idea is to make the dog happy to do something different instead, and not scare it into depression or even worse, attack.

Care into their Senior Years

The one fault that our dogs have is that they get old far too soon.

As they age, many fit and healthy Aussies of all sizes can carry on in competitive agility and similar sports. This is a throwback from their genetic history, as herding breeds were expected to work into their senior years.

Because it is quite a robust little dog, and with no health problems, the Mini Australian Shepherd is a usual sight in agility circles right up to their tenth birthday and beyond.

Although they have a life expectancy of between 12-13 years, it is not unheard of for Mini Aussies to still enjoy long family hikes into their teens. Yet at some point every dog, no matter how healthy, will be ready for rest and a quiet retirement.

Time goes by so fast and when you have followed accurate training and behavior advice you will have settled into a good routine where everyone knows how to behave and you live together happily. Next thing you know your dog is slowing down and may even be going a little grey.

The Mini Aussie never really gets old in its thoughts. Their mind will stay pretty active right into its senior years, and therefore gentle dog training will benefit even the most mature Australian Shepherd.

As your dog gets older you may find that they need some extra help to stay healthy. It may need its ears cleaning more regularly or a tartar removal on its teeth due to excess build up.

This small dog may even develop joint problems and need help in the form of natural remedies or veterinary treatment to live a long and healthy life.

Some great natural remedies for stiff joints are fish oils and glucosamine. Green lipped muscle too can have great results.

Be sure to look up dosage amounts for the size of your dog before using anything like this.

Another thing you may find when your Aussie gets older is that it becomes a bit confused by any change. The dog may pace on stiff legs or become more yappy than usual.

This is old age setting in and dogs, like people, can certainly suffer with a form of dementia. This can be delayed by keeping your dog's mind active and teaching simple tricks and commands plus regular walks where they use as many senses as possible.

You may also come to a point where one or more of your dog's senses begin to fade. Either their sight or hearing could come into question. If it is their hearing you might even find yourself wondering whether they are going deaf or just ignoring you.

Toilet training may also suffer because they can't get to the door quick enough, or last through the night.

These senior years with your dog are magical in themselves. These times dictate a completely different type of relationship and one that you should cherish.

The dog that offered you all of its youth, with enthusiasm and gusto, now needs extra love. They might want to sleep for longer or refuse a rainy walk on the odd day, or it may not.

One thing is for certain, the dog that grows old with you offers a whole lifetime of gathered love. So when your Aussie stares at you, despite all their needs having been met, or pees on the floor in the night because its bladder is weak, it's up to you to remember that they can't help it.

In these more vulnerable years they need your patience and extra love, for they have no choice but to grow old.

Saying Goodbye

The main difference between losing a dog and a person is that often, with a dog, we often have to make the decision to end their life when it is suffering.

We struggle with this because we want to choose the right time. We do not want to rob our beloved pet of one more day in the sun and similarly we do not want to burden them with unnecessary pain.

Whether you make the choice of euthanasia if your dog is suffering, or you lose him quickly in an unexpected way, it still hurts and will hurt for a long time to come.

I wanted to add this section in at the end of the book to give you some understanding about the process when you choose euthanasia as an option, and you think it's time.

When you have had a lifetime with a dog, you should also have a good relationship with your veterinarian. Therefore either you or the vet will begin to gently suggest that it's time. I think it is only fair at this point that I explain to you what happens when it is time for a dog to say goodbye. So many people do not know what to expect.

When the decision is made to help a dog out of its suffering, then the vet will administer an overdose of anesthetic. The dog will simply go to sleep and does not suffer. It is usually the choice of the dog's owner whether this is carried out at home, on a planned visit, or at the surgery.

A good vet will usually sedate the dog first so that the pet does not need to go through the process of the vet finding a vein whilst it is awake. Within seconds of the dog going to sleep they will be gone.

Many owners feed their dog with something super tasty at the last minute and then hold their dog tight as it dies.

Some owners find it difficult to be there at the time of euthanasia. Yet we owe the loyal dog our strength and reassurance because we can cry afterwards, but at the time we need to be strong for the sake of our friend. When it's time to say goodbye to your dog you will find the strength from somewhere.

The grief will come after the shock.

We grieve in a particularly harsh way for a beloved pet; this is because the dog is usually always there.

They listen to our worries, cheer us up after a hard day, and lick our tears away when we cry.

Then suddenly the place that was previously filled with a warm body is vacant, and our lives feel empty.

You may feel like you will never get over your loss, but you will.

You may still cry over your dog but when the grief begins to fade your happy memories will begin to filter through.

The cheeky things that your Aussie did, or a gaze that will be etched into your mind forever more, will replace your sadness, when you least expect it.

Useful Links

Kennel Clubs and Rescue

www.mascaonline.com

www.ukmasc.com

www.akc.org

www.thekennelclub.org.uk

www.miniaussierescue.org

Pets Travel Scheme

www.gov.uk/take-pet-abroad/overview

Activity and Health

dogblog.ruffwear.net

blog.k9active.co.uk

www.agilitynet.com

www.usdaa.com

www.flyball.org.uk

www.flyball.org

cani-cross.co.uk

www.nsarda.co.uk

ardainc.org

www.adaptil.com/uk

www.bachflower.com/rescue-remedy-information

Index